Canal Fishing

Pan Anglers' Library

Canal Fishing

Kenneth Seaman

Pan Books London and Sydney

First published 1971 by Barrie & Jenkins Ltd
This edition published 1973 by Pan Books Ltd,
Cavaye Place, London SW10 9PG
2nd printing 1976
© Kenneth Seaman 1971
ISBN 0 330 23511 7
Made and printed in Great Britain by
Cox & Wyman Ltd, London, Reading and Fakenham

CONTENTS

Introduction

Canal fishing has received scant attention from most angling writers, and it was with the intention of filling this gap that I undertook the writing of this book. Some of the methods described will be familiar to most anglers and can be used successfully in other similar man-made waters, such as drains and dykes. Other methods may not be as familiar, and may even seem unusual to some; but all of them have been tried and proved. If used in those circumstances and conditions for which they were designed, they will not only help the canal angler to catch fish but may widen the scope of his technique and increase his enjoyment too. Canal fishing has for too long been associated with a certain almost ritualized style of fishing. In this book, I have attempted to reveal that it need not always be so.

It may appear that angling for roach has been given an excessive amount of space; but as these are the most numerous, most sought-after and most important fish, I feel that I have only given the species the attention it deserves. Other fish there certainly are, some of which few anglers ever seek deliberately. I hope I have at least opened the door to reveal some of the excitements and thrills that can be enjoyed by those who cast a line into these much maligned and neglected waters.

The greater part of the writing in this book is naturally related to my own experience, but I would like to thank Jim Gibbinson for his contribution to the chapter on eel fishing; Trevor Housby for his contribution to the chapter on rudd fishing; the British Waterways Board for general information about canals; and lastly, *Angling Times* for permission to use extracts from news items from that paper.

CHAPTER 1

Different Canals and the Angler's Problems

A man who wishes to become a successful horticulturist must first learn how plants grow; what they need for their sustenance; how they are influenced by their environment. He must learn how to get the best from his soil. Similarly, the angler who aspires to become good at his chosen art must learn about fish and about the environment in which they live. He must understand that this environment exerts a profound influence upon the feeding habits and growth rates of fish, and that all environments differ to some degree from each other.

Canals are no exception. At first sight, they may look featureless. The banks often run in an undeviating line for several miles. The water has no distinguishing features of fast and slow water that are so common in rivers, except below the lock gates. It is difficult at first to know where to start and how best to fish. It takes time and experience to get the best from a canal. The beginner may have to learn slowly. He cannot make a better start than to walk along its banks, plumb the water, ask questions of those who know it well, and thus equip himself with a basic knowledge of the water upon which he can build his own construction of ideas, methods, baits and tackle.

The first thing he will learn is that although all canals may look alike they are as different from each other as one member of a family group is from another. Some canals have waters of marvellous clarity, in which you may sometimes see huge shoals of roach and other fish. Other canals are murky, greenish-coloured waters in which the fish remain largely invisible.

The bottom formation of these canals is often different too, and this difference inevitably leads to a varied reed-growth. In most canals, the deepest part lies roughly down the centre. The fringes of such canals are often thickly lined with emergent reeds. Only the 'boat-road' – the channel kept clear by barges and other boats – is really fishable. In other canals, only the tow-path side is shallow and reedy; the deeper water might lie nearer to the far bank and extend roughly two-thirds of the way across. Yet other canals have become silted up, their original outlines blurred. If the water is very clear, as it often is, the reed-growth in such canals is usually extensive and includes both emergent and underwater growths. They might even become so overgrown that most anglers would regard them as unfishable. (See Figs 1, 2 and 3.)

In most canals, the efforts of the local River Board keep large areas of water comparatively free from reeds. Such areas will be easily accessible but hard-fished, and the fish will be more difficult to catch. Canal anglers who aspire to catch the better fish should learn not to always seek the easiest places but to think instead where the fish might be, taking into account the nature of the water and the conditions prevailing at the time.

Fish in canals – especially roach, which are the most prolific and most sought-after fish – move about a great deal and will not always be found in the same place. This fact goes part of the way towards explaining why it is that a spot which produces good roach one day will not necessarily produce them the next. The roach might still be there, but not feeding. Alternatively, they may have been scared away or have moved off. Where they go is a puzzle to which the canal angler may seldom find a satisfactory answer unless he can see them.

It is possible, however, to go part way towards finding a solution. We can often determine where the fish will *not* be, in view of the conditions. Basking fish can usually be ignored. They are not likely to feed. But if the fish cannot be seen and the sun is on the water, they are most likely to be found in the deepest part of the canal or hidden in the reeds, where they can shelter from the sun. They will not usually be in the shallows or close to the tow-path, where the concentration of anglers and noise is at its peak.

The discerning angler will recognize this and fish his bait at the edge of the reeds in the deep water of the centre channel or, in the case of the clear-water canal, across under the far bank, where he expects the fish to be lying. And he will be right, more often than not, if he does this. A bait fished in the shallow water, close to the tow-path, is not likely to tempt many fish.

On the other hand, an overcast sky and a stiff inshore

Figure 1. Canal with deep boat-road and extensive marginal reed

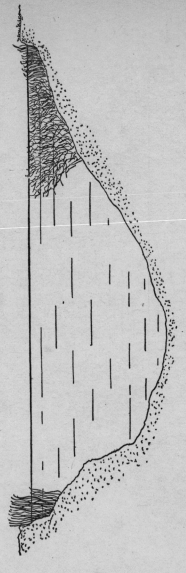

Figure 2. Typical canal with deeper water near to the far bank

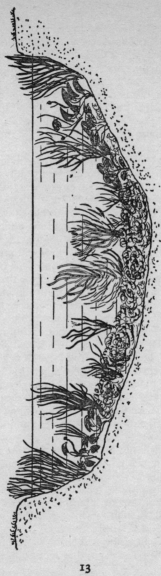

Figure 3. Canal showing effects of silting and neglect

breeze may bring the fish close to the angler – even close in to the bank from which he is fishing, if there is a sufficient depth of water there. When the surface mirror is broken by the wind, the angler is not as conspicuous. The fish often move in to feed on the shelf, where the water begins to shallow off and there is a gently sloping bank upon which natural food can be found. If the fish can be kept there, they can probably be caught. The intervening beds of reeds, where they exist, should not be regarded as a handicap. They provide cover for the angler. A long rod will enable him to reach out over them. He may catch more fish than he would if the water were completely reedless.

The angler has to think about the condition of the canal bottom, too, if he hopes to get the best results possible from his water. Is it composed of clay or gravel? Or is it composed of mud? Is there reed or no reed? These questions need to be answered before he can rig up his tackle efficiently. A mud bottom will make orthodox bottom fishing difficult – a waste of time, even – for it will probably obscure his bait from the fish; and if they have to dig for it, they will probably pass it by. So the thoughtful angler will first find out about the nature of the canal bottom. If it is muddy or thick with reeds, then he will not fish his bait hard on the bottom. Acting on the premise that a visible bait is ten times more likely to catch fish than one that is hidden, he will arrange his tackle so that the bait does not fall right on to the bottom but just skims it at maximum fall. Or he will use a bait which he knows will remain visible to the fish; a piece of crust or flake, perhaps.

A much different situation exists where the bottom of the canal is composed of clay or gravel. The angler may be able to see the bottom and even the fish. If so, then a choice of methods is his. He can fish his bait in a slow-sinking style and take his fish 'on the drop'; or, if he has ambitions for better fish, he may choose to leger his bait lightly on the bottom, knowing that it will not be hidden in the bottom debris and that a good fish may find and take it. In these circumstances, he may even be able to watch the fish take the bait.

Where there is a more formidable combination of mud bottom and thick masses of submerged reed, the question the angler has to ask himself is whether such a spot is worth fishing at all and, if it is, what methods he can use to tempt fish and keep his bait visible and his tackle free from snags. If there are any fish in the swim, they may be in the reeds – in which case, he must fish his bait in them, either in the pockets of clear water or resting on the reeds. It must lie there lightly, so that the fish can see it and pick it up without fear. If, on the other hand, the fish are lying above the reeds at mid-water level, then he must adjust his tackle to allow his bait to fall down to them but not into the bottom-hugging reeds. He must work for his fish, and fish carefully to avoid scaring them out of his swim. With luck, if the sun is up, he may see them, and also see how his bait acts and at what level in the water it is taken. If not, then he must use his knowledge of the canal to make a fine judgement about his tackle set-up and the depth at which he will fish his bait. Angling in canals is not always easy.

If and when the reed-cutters work through the canal, a further problem will confront him. Superficially, the water may seem to have been improved. The surface reed has been removed; the water looks clear and inviting. But it hides many traps for the unwary in the form of shorn-off roots of reeds. These may ensnare his hook and bait. He will waste much time freeing his tackle; trying to find a clean spot; striking at false bites caused by the protruding remnants of reed on the canal bottom. The areas of clear water, once so unmistakably defined, have been obscured. His cover has gone, too. He must find a way to fish over the reeds, and to angle without sitting in plain view of the fish. He may wish the reed-cutters had not come.

In the natural course of events, he will gradually learn how to overcome these problems. His greatest difficulty will remain that of singling out one species of fish from another. Quite possibly, he will not think too deeply about this but will be content to take whatever comes his way. This is fishing, of a kind. But it is not as satisfying as fishing that is specifically aimed at catching a certain species or even a specific fish.

It must be admitted that it is not easy to do this. In the seemingly featureless waters of a canal, there are no well-defined swims like there are in rivers; no places which one can pinpoint as belonging almost exclusively to one species. Because of this, the business of fishing selectively becomes much more difficult than it is in rivers. Yet the keen angler will not let this deter him from trying. He will learn gradually that certain species can be caught most easily at certain times of the year – or day, even; that certain combinations of baits and methods will yield the kind of fish he wants to catch, more often than not; and that fish can often be taken from the surface, as well as at mid-water level and right on the bottom. Success will not come easily; but come it will, if he persists, and if he is not put off by the fact that he will often catch nothing and will thus appear to fail. It is comparatively easy to catch anything; not so easy to catch certain species. But therein lies the essential difference between fishing and angling.

The passing of the seasons brings changes to the canal. As autumn merges into winter, the reeds begin to wither and die. The bottom of the canal becomes covered with decaying vegetation, which can foul and obscure a bait carelessly fished on the bottom. The water often becomes murky – inhospitable looking. The temperature drops. Cold days and colder nights lie ahead; the frosts and snow of winter carpet the banks and silver the water with ice. Fish become harder to catch. Faint hearts begin to desert the canal banks. Only the true stalwarts fish on. The experienced angler can still catch fish. There will be many mild days during the winter and spring months to look forward to.

Meanwhile, the angler will use his knowledge of the canal and its fish to achieve some measure of success, even though the conditions may seem to be against him. No longer will he fish as keenly for tench, or rudd, or bream. Instead, he will concentrate on those fish which experience has taught him must offer the best chances of sport: pike, perch and, above all, roach. Now that the reeds have died away, the water will be much clearer. There will be more opportunity to use a spinner or dead-bait. He can keep warm and interested by searching for his fish instead of waiting for them to come to him.

He will also know that roach will now be found mainly in the deeper water and that the later hours of the day will be better than the early hours, which he used to such telling effect during the summer when the boat traffic was at its peak. The water may be clearer, devoid of cover; but by way of compensation, the fishes' natural larder is not now as abundantly supplied as it once was. There will be days when roach will be looking for food and will bite freely. The angler may even find that he can break the ice and still catch roach. Low temperatures are not as detrimental to the angler's chances as many seem to think.

Indeed, the angler who has learned to understand his canal

and has made a study of it and its fish will not be unduly apprehensive about the winter. He will already know where to fish, at what times and on which species he ought to concentrate.

There are many fish and many ways of catching them. The canal angler must be every bit as versatile as the river angler, his repertoire of methods and baits just as extensive.

CHAPTER 2

Tackle

The most important item of the canal angler's equipment is his rod. This is the tool he must use to cast his bait, strike with and land his fish. Until comparatively recently, such a rod would have been stiff in action, with only a flexible tip. It would have been constructed of whole cane, greenheart or Spanish reed; its length usually twelve to fourteen feet. Its function was to cast a small lightly weighted bait across the canal and whip out, in a minimum of time, any fish caught. Little thought was ever given to the needs of the specimen hunter or the specialist. Rods were built to suit the needs of an angling public firmly held in the grip of tradition. The cult of 'fine and far off' was unchallenged by all but a few individuals whose voices were seldom, if ever, heard. Canal anglers were mostly working-class men with little money to spare, fishing with a shop-built rod if they could afford it – a bamboo cane, obtainable for a few pence – or perhaps a willow or ash-plant cut from the hedge.

My earliest canal fishing was done with a fourteen-foot cane, a cheap braided line and a halfpenny hook to gut. The line was tied to the end of the cane, and the float – usually a home-made one, improvised from a pigeon or crow quill – was attached to the line with two rubber bands. No reel was used. Our style was tight line, with the float almost under the rod-tip; and the tackle was usually strong enough to hoist a roach out over the reeds without the aid of a landing net. Later, we graduated to three-piece rods of whole cane and wooden reels – usually given away by an older angler who had graduated to more expensive equipment.

Very few metal reels were in evidence then. The Nottingham-style wooden reel was in vogue. Some of these reels revealed a very high standard of workmanship – smooth-running, smoothly polished to the appearance of dark metal, and reinforced with strips of brass. In the hands of experts, long casts across to the far bank appeared like child's play. The lines used then were usually cheap braided ones, or silk. Both had to be greased to make them float. The lightness and better floating qualities of the silk lines made them firm favourites. The monofilaments used by today's anglers were unheard of, as were the modern fixed-spool reels.

Canal anglers of bygone days were not usually finicky about their choice of floats either. The learned discussions on 'resistance', 'drag' and 'inertia' that are sometimes aired in angling journals today were unheard of. Possibly, a large number of these anglers fished clumsily and inefficiently by today's standards. The large quill floats used by some of them would make many modern exponents of the 'fine and far off' technique shudder with horror. But they caught fish. Some of them caught more fish, and bigger fish, than their present-day counterparts. Not having the advantage of the modern loaded float and the ease of casting that can be achieved with the fixed-spool reel, they had to attain distance casting and lightness of presentation by careful shotting and skilful use of the centre-pin reel.

By way of compensation, canals were better in many ways then. There was little or no pollution. The waters were not as over-fished and overcrowded as they are now. The fish were probably easier to catch, too, with the average size in most canals larger than it is today. Anglers often kept their catches. Match fishing had yet to reach its peak.

Nowadays, the breed of canal angler that once sat patiently along the banks of the local 'cut' has practically vanished. In its place has sprung up a new breed: men who are wealthier, better-equipped, more mobile and largely match-conscious, but who often still cling faithfully to the techniques evolved by the old masters. The equipment has changed but the basic traditional style remains largely intact. The superior design and finish of the modern canal angler's equipment only makes easier the art of casting and striking. Most of the fish he catches are still small, still caught in the 'fine and far off' style.

Accordingly, most of the rods perform precisely the same function as those used by the old-timers; but they are undoubtedly of superior construction and strength. They are usually twelve feet to fourteen and a half feet in length, and of such flexibility that the finest of lines can be used. But a minority of canal anglers has moved even further. New materials, such as fibre-glass, together with individual preferences in length and construction, have resulted in many new and different rods appearing on the scene. A walk along a canal bank would reveal a variety of rods in use, ranging from whole-cane with a built-cane tip, through to completely built-cane, fibre-glass and even steel. Each angler will have his individual preference. He may be merely aping a well-known master whose exploits have been associated with a certain type of rod. He may have been subconsciously pressurized into buying by skilful advertising. A rod may just have caught his eye. Anglers are human. The aesthetic appeal of a rod sometimes overshadows its quality as an efficient piece of equipment. Whatever his motive, the canal angler is likely to maintain that his choice is the best for his kind of fishing or for his canal.

It is extremely doubtful, though, whether one rod is sufficient to meet all the needs of the specialist canal angler. If he is to angle successfully for all species of fish in the many different conditions he will encounter in canals, the range of his rods and tackle must be extended. The rod and tackle that is quite adequate for angling for small fish in clear waters may prove entirely inadequate for dealing with the larger fish of the overgrown waters. This problem cannot always be solved by the simple expedient of changing to a stronger line. The rod must often be changed, too. Specialized fishing demands specialized equipment.

For general use, a twelve-foot to fourteen-and-a-half-foot flexible rod of built-cane or fibre-glass is ideal for use with lines of a low breaking strain. For close-range fishing, and for legering for larger fish in overgrown waters, a stronger type of rod is advisable. I often use my Mark IV Avon – a ten-foot built-cane rod which can be used with lines in the five-pound to eight-pound breaking-strain range – which is ideal for handling chub, tench, bream and large roach in these difficult conditions. I also find use for a light brook-type fly-rod, eight and a half feet in length; a nine-and-a-half-foot fly-rod for chub; a spinning-rod for perch fishing; and also a pike rod that can be used for spinning and live-baiting. My own is ten feet long, and made of built-cane.

There are also many excellent glass rods on the market now, although some years ago there was a widely held prejudice against them. Glass rods are strong, virtually unbreakable, and are available in many different sizes and designs. The important point is to choose a rod that will perform the task for which it is designed. Serious damage can result from using rods for purposes for which they are not designed.

Lines

Canal angling is synonymous with fine-line fishing. The average angler would shudder at any suggestion that he could use a line of greater breaking-strain than two pounds. For many, a one-pound to one-and-a-half-pound breaking-strain line is regarded as a necessity. My own experience has taught me otherwise. Fine lines may be essential for certain styles of fishing, but they are not always indispensable. In fact, in some cases the use of a fine line could be disastrous. Nevertheless, strongly held opinions about the necessity for fine lines cannot be dismissed lightly.

I think there are several reasons for this belief in them. One of these must be the influence of habit and tradition. Canal fishing has always been associated with angling for small fish with fine tackle, and once an idea has become universally accepted its veracity is seldom challenged. Another reason is that fine lines usually result in more bites when the slow-sinking style of fishing is used. Objections to stronger lines are usually based mainly upon the fear that the fish will see the line and will be put off from taking the bait. But I doubt very much whether fish are capable of such fine discrimination. If they can see one line, they can see another. I doubt if there is any line they cannot see, in normal conditions.

The true reason why less fish are caught with a slow-sinking bait fished on a strong line might rather be that it is not as pliable as a line of lower breaking strain. Consequently, the bait does not fall through the water as naturally as one fished on a fine line. Since the majority of canal anglers use a slow-sinking style, an undeserved prejudice has grown up against the strong line.

It would be true to say that even this legitimate objection to the strong line can be overcome to a great extent by using a larger hook and a bigger bait. This can be proved by experiment. If a small hook is tied to a strong line and baited with a maggot, its sinking action in a vessel of water will appear slow and unnatural; but tie on a large hook and bait it with a lobworm or a knob of cheese, and the bait will fall through the water in a much more natural manner. It increases the chance that the bait will be taken, and the supposed scaring effect that the line has on the fish will be largely negated. This I have proved to myself over and over again by catching numerous canal roach and other fish while using strong lines and large hooks. The strong line is really most suitable for bottom fishing, though. Since the bait and part of the line are lying along the bottom, the question of unnatural action of the bait does not arise. Fine lines are most suitable for catching small fish, stronger lines for catching the larger ones. I have a place for both in my tackle box.

The colour of the line is of some importance, too, I think. Transparent or pearl-coloured lines seem to reflect too much light, and when the sun is on the water they can often be seen quite clearly. Does this unnatural glint of reflected light have a scaring effect on the fish? I feel that it does. For this reason, I tend to use green-coloured lines. A small point, perhaps; but if it leads to more fish in the net, then it is worth thinking about. The successful angler is often successful because he attends to small points that others neglect.

Hooks

The same kind of prejudice that excludes strong lines from the tackle boxes of most anglers also deters them from using large hooks. Sizes 16, 18 and 20 are considered normal for canal fishing. The idea of using a size, 10, 8 or even 6 is seldom considered because it is thought that the fish will see the big hook and refuse the bait. Again, this is only partly true. It would not be wise to use a maggot on a big hook or a lobworm on a small hook. The maxim should be a small hook for a small bait and a large hook for a large bait. I often use a size 6 or 8 hook for my canal fishing. I do not consider such hooks big when seeking chub or roach and using a big bait. My tackle box contains hooks ranging from size 18 to size 4, and I find use for all of them. Anyone who is still sceptical might like to reflect upon the experience of Jim Gibbinson, the well-known member of the National Anguilla Club, and his friends. While fishing the Grand Union Canal for eels, they caught roach, chub and perch on hooks up to size 2, mounted on fifteen-pound breaking-strain braided wire. Admittedly, these fish were caught during the night and with a bait lying along the bottom; but such experience does indicate that fine lines and small hooks are not as necessary as most canal anglers believe.

This kind of tackle would not catch many fish during daylight hours, though; and it certainly would not be suitable for normal canal-fishing styles, for which the line should be supple and the hooks of fine wire, and sharp. The old style hook-to-gut has been replaced by hook-to-nylon, which is preferred by the majority of canal anglers now; but spade-end and eyed hooks are used too. The very small hooks, sizes 16 to 22, are designed to catch small fish and are most suitable for use with maggots and casters. The main requirements are that they should be of wire and very sharp, so that they will not damage the bait.

The same principles should be applied in the choice of larger hooks. They are more suitable for the bigger fish because they have greater strength, give a firmer hook hold and are less likely to pull out. I have a personal preference for spade-ends, except when seeking chub. Most eyed hooks are too heavy, the eyes too large. This is a matter of some importance to the canal angler because the heavy hook causes the bait to descend at a faster rate than with the fine-wire hook, and fish may be missed when fishing a slowly descending bait. This does not apply to the same degree when fishing the bait on the bottom or in strong currents, but in the still and clear waters of some canals it could be a matter of crucial importance.

Every precaution should be taken to ensure that the bait is presented as attractively as possible. Hooks are comparatively cheap. Any hook that looks defective or crude, or which has become distorted, should be discarded. Never use a blunt hook or a damaged hook. It is a false economy.

Floats

Floats are another important item of the canal angler's equipment. A wide variety of floats is obtainable, and the beginner could easily become confused at the multiplicity of floats that are arranged to catch his eye in the tackle shops. Very few of them embody all the qualities that an ideal canal float should have. Such an ideal would be difficult to attain because a float which would be suitable for every condition of water and weather would have to combine sensitivity, weight, lightness, stability and visibility at long range. What is possible is to select a small range of floats which will meet most, if not all, of these requirements.

The subject of floats and their suitability is a controversial matter involving aspects of float behaviour such as drag, inertia and sensitivity. It is all highly technical, and it can become confusing. I think the best way to assess the effectiveness of any float is to start at that point where its action matters most – beneath the water, the way the fish sees and feels it.

Ideally, the fish should feel little or no resistance from the float: so if we choose a float that even the tiniest of fish can move, we need have few qualms about whether the fish will feel any resistance from it. This is important. If a fish has to move an object that offers detectable resistance, it will probably release the bait quickly; and since our own reactions are not generally quick enough to strike before this happens, the fish will be missed.

I learned how to overcome this problem when I was very young by using a float that, when weighted with a grain of malt or a small blob of paste, would cock and sink until only its tip was showing. It would be difficult indeed to reduce float resistance any further without dispensing with the float altogether. Such floats are not difficult to find or make. I fashioned mine out of fowl and pigeon quills. A whole range of easily made, ridiculously cheap floats can be made from these quills. Each one should be a little larger than the other. I had dozens of them. The slightest touch from a feeding roach or even a gudgeon would sink them.

Other excellent canal floats can be made from porcupine and peacock quills, obtainable from any reputable tackle shop. Porcupine quills are favourites of mine. They are dark-coloured, reversible and tough. Peacock quills can be cut to almost any size, and they make excellent 'lift' floats as well as being extremely useful for normal swimming-down methods.

Quill floats can also be easily transformed into self-cockers by winding lead wire around the base of the float or, in the case of the hollow fowl quills, by cutting them open and inserting a few weights. Whenever this is done, they should be carefully resealed with glue and then painted and varnished to ensure that they are watertight; otherwise, they will soon become waterlogged and will sink.

Such floats, or a similar shop-bought variety, are much used by canal anglers. So are the small self-cockers. Some of these are made from elder pith or balsa wood, and they have the necessary weight built in to them. Both are excellent floats of their kind; but of the two, the balsa float is the more durable. Pith floats are fragile and easily broken. Self-cockers are used extensively for far-bank fishing. 'Zoomer' floats are also widely used by many canal anglers. Their streamlined shape makes them ideal for effortless casting across the canal (Fig 4).

In my opinion, none of these floats can rival the simple quill for delicacy of presentation and sensitivity. The deficiency of the quill lies in its lightness, which makes long casting difficult – especially when fishing into the wind. In such conditions the zoomer-type float or a self-cocker is a better choice. The antenna float – which has a long, thin, spine tip – is also a useful float when the canal is ruffled by a strong breeze, especially when a bottom-fishing style is used, because the thin spine offers negligible wind resistance and the

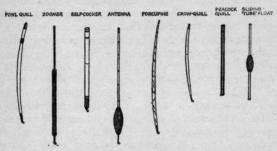

Figure 4. A selection of popular canal fishing floats

float does not drift out of position. These floats can be bought in various sizes, but the larger ones are not suitable for canal fishing. Only the smaller ones, requiring a minimum of shot, are needed. These can be made from balsa wood or cane; and some anglers prefer to 'do it themselves', producing beautiful floats of their own design. Various shades of colouring are used. I favour a dark green body with a yellow or orange tip. Black is a useful alternative which shows up surprisingly well in most conditions.

The appearance of the float is relatively unimportant, though. The angler's first consideration should be whether it is most suitable for the task he has in mind. A carefully chosen float can add many fish to the total catch; a badly designed and badly chosen float can reduce his catch, or even ruin his chances altogether. As an illustration, there was the occasion when I watched two anglers fishing in a local canal. One was using a tiny self-cocker and netting fish after fish. The other was using a large float which I could see easily, even though I was more than twenty yards away. In around six hours of fishing, he failed to catch a single fish. Quite possibly, factors other than float size contributed to his failure; but I am quite sure that the float, which would have required a substantial pull from a large fish to sink it, played no small part in it.

Use the smallest float possible in the prevailing conditions and you will not go far wrong. On those rare occasions when I have arrived on the canal bank without a float, I have used a twig. If this is cut carefully and used with the thickest end down and its tip stripped of bark, it makes an excellent self-cocker. Other anglers might laugh at such a float. The fish won't, though. As long as the presentation is right and the float resistance negligible, the fact that the bait is suspended beneath a common twig instead of a finely made float will not deter the fish from taking it.

Weights

Weights are important to the canal angler. Generally speaking, the larger Swan shot and BB shot are not required – except, perhaps, for legering. A liberal supply of soft split shot, ranging from AA to dust shot, should suffice. This shot should be soft and dull. Hard shot requires more force to tighten it on to the line, and may cause damage. Bright shot is a fish-scarer.

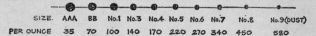

SIZE.	AAA	BB	No.1	No.3	No.4	No.5	No.6	No.7	No.8	No.9 (DUST)
PER OUNCE	35	70	100	140	170	220	270	340	450	580

Figure 5. A selection of split shot. The figures indicate approximate size and number per ounce

Drilled shot can be made use of, too. There are places in canals, notably in the races and in the turbulent water below the lock gates, where such weights can be used. The heavier half-ounce to two-ounce leger weights which are used for long-casting purposes in still waters and rivers are seldom, if ever, needed for normal canal fishing.

Lead foil is useful and is preferred by some anglers since it can be folded around the line. There is less risk of breakage than there is when using split shot.

Small swivels also make very useful running weights (Fig 5).

Reels

The type of reel most favoured now is undoubtedly the fixed-spool reel. Centre-pins are used only rarely by most canal anglers. The fixed-spool is simple to use and enables long casts to be made with the merest flick of the wrist, provided that the spool is well filled. This is a matter which should not be neglected. Efficient casting is impossible if it is not attended to. Ideally, the spool should be filled to within one-eighth of an inch of its rim. Overfilling can cause 'birds' nests' – horrible tangles of overlapping coils of line. Underfilling drastically reduces casting distance. With a well-filled spool of fine line within the one-and-a-half to three-pound breaking-strain range, it is possible, under normal conditions, to cast a tiny quill float clear across a canal. Rod, line and float must be regarded as one unit which will only operate at maximum efficiency if each complements and works smoothly in conjunction with the other.

The casting is often done with a sweeping, overhead motion of the rod – the line being released from the spool at that precise moment when float and line have been projected across the canal. Personally, I favour the underhand or sideways cast. If the rod has action right down to the butt and the spool is well filled, little difficulty should be experienced in casting the lightest of floats many yards. A few experts can do this with centre-pin reels; but for quickness and ease of operation, the fixed-spool must be preferred.

Leger-stops

Leger-stops are used to prevent the link which has the weights attached to it from sliding down to the hook. The most commonly used stop is the split shot, which is effective but does lead to line weakness through compression of the line. Another form of stop is a small piece of valve-rubber or electric cable flex. The line is threaded through this twice to form an effective stop. Some anglers use a split ring or a small swivel. The only fault with these is that the line must be tied to them, and this means knots which tend to weaken the line. A half-blood knot is favoured for attaching the line to these stops.

Lastly, there is the plastic leger-stop, which is finding favour with many anglers and which was kindly passed on to me by Peter Wheat. It is quite a simple but effective arrangement, consisting of a small plastic tube through which the line is passed and then held in position by inserting another, smaller tube. The same effect can be achieved by using a piece of cable flex and a matchstick, which swells up in the water and holds the line firmly.

All of these stops are illustrated in Chapter V, Figure 13.

Other Tackle

The following additional items of equipment are useful: a selection of thick rubber bands, and float-caps of different colours; a selection of swivels for legering and spinning; a disgorger and a pair of artery forceps for extracting hooks; wire-traces of varying strengths for live-baiting and spinning; a bait-can for retaining minnows and other live baits; a keep-net; a rod-rest; a landing net; a gaff; a small selection of flies and nymphs; and a stout waterproof sheet. Those who put their comfort first might prefer a basket or a stool to sit on. I use neither preferring to sit low on the bank on a plastic sheet. I am sure this preference for keeping low and concealed has enabled me to catch a great many fish I might not otherwise have caught.

CHAPTER 3

Baits

Maggots

The most popular bait used by canal anglers today must be maggots. Every known species of fish will take them, and some anglers use little else throughout the season. The most popular maggots are probably 'gozzers' – a strain carefully bred in the flesh of dead game birds – and 'annato' maggots, which are usually bred in hearts impregnated with annato dye. 'Squats' and 'pinkies' are smaller maggots used almost solely for groundbaiting.

Breeding these maggots is a specialist's job which should not be attempted by the amateur until he has acquainted himself with all the necessary related information. Laws exist regarding the breeding of maggots. If they are contravened, prosecution can result.

The normal colouring of maggots is white or pale yellow, but they can be dyed various colours. The most popular colours are pink and yellow. Blue and green maggots can be obtained too. Coloured maggots look more attractive to the human eye, but whether or not fish find them so is a matter for conjecture. Experiments conducted by research workers indicate that fish have a wider range of visual achievement than is generally believed, so the appeal of coloured maggots cannot be altogether discounted. Nevertheless, the angler using maggots should concentrate on size and liveliness rather than colour. Fish are stimulated more by movement and size than they are by colour. A fat, soft and lively maggot will usually take more fish than a small, tough maggot, irrespective of its colour. Odour is important too. Most maggots are greasy and have an unpleasant smell. They should be cleaned several times in bran before use and then kept in a large tin with plenty of holes in the lid.

The question of liveliness is closely linked with the manner in which a maggot is impaled on the hook. If the maggot is killed, its lack of movement will make it less attractive. It should be hooked lightly through the skin, and the point of the hook should be revealed. The fish will not normally be put off by this if the hook is small and sharp. Sizes 14, 16 or 18 should be used for single-maggot fishing. A larger hook can be used for fishing double maggots or a bunch of them. As long as the hook is sharp and fine, the maggots will retain their essential liveliness for some time. As soon as they are dead, or have been sucked dry of their juices by a fish, they should be removed and replaced by fresh maggots. Fish will sometimes bite at skins and dead maggots; but there can be no doubt that a lively maggot is far more killing. Some canal anglers remove the maggot and replace it with a fresh one if they simply miss a bite. This might seem to be carrying fastidiousness too far – but there is evidence to suggest that roach and dace often shy away from a maggot that has been bitten and rejected by another fish.

The quantity of maggots needed is another important point. Normally, good catches of fish cannot be expected unless a reasonable quantity of maggots are taken to be used as hook-baits and feeders. Some anglers take gallons, and use them all. Most use the pinkies as feeders and the larger maggots as hook-baits, the idea being that the pinkies will attract fish which will then prefer the larger maggots on the hook. I am not sure that this desired reaction always takes place. The liberal use of small maggots also attracts hordes of small fish. Small maggots sink more slowly than the larger ones and are thus more vulnerable to attack from the small fish. The angler seeking a better class of fish might be well advised to ponder upon the desirability of any action which encourages small fish into his swim, and then use his maggots accordingly.

In my experience, the angler who uses large maggots exclusively, both on his hook and mixed in with his groundbait, will usually catch better fish than the angler who uses small maggots. One cannot lay down fixed rules about this since other factors connected with the presentation of the bait and the choice of swim are involved. There can be no doubt, though, that maggots are the best bait for the angler seeking a mixed bag of fish. On the other hand, they can be – somewhat paradoxically – the worst bait for the angler who has a specific kind of fish in mind. There is a wide choice of other baits, any one of which might suit his purpose better.

Casters

Casters rival maggots for pride of place in the canal angler's list of favourite baits, and some anglers prefer them. In some quarters, they have been hailed as a new wonder-bait, requiring all kinds of specialized skills to fish them successfully. The beginner should not let this deter him from using them. Chrysalids have been used by discerning anglers for a great many years now; and there is more than one way of using them, as I shall presently reveal.

Quite simply, casters are chrysalids in the early stage of their development into flies. At first, the chrysalids are pale yellow and soft. Later, they darken to a red-brown colour and finally to black, when they become hard and brittle. They are at their most deadly in the early stages, when they will sink in water. A day or so later they will float, and are then known as 'floaters'. The maggots do not all 'turn' simultaneously, but there is always a certain proportion in roughly the same stage of development.

Floaters are sorted out from casters by placing the chrysalids in a bucket of water. The floaters can then be skimmed off. They are often thrown away; but I do not throw mine away. They can be a deadly bait for roach and dace, and chub too, sometimes. When separated, the casters should be retained in a cool place – in a refrigerator, if the weather is very warm – otherwise they will rapidly turn into flies. These, too, can be a deadly bait for surface-feeding fish; but if the chrysalids are needed, their development must be arrested. This is vital.

The beauty of fishing with casters is that they sink by their own weight alone. They should be fished on a small, sharp hook – size 16 or 18. Some anglers attach them like maggots, hooked lightly through the blunt end, with the point of the hook showing. Others maintain that the hook should be entirely hidden in the caster. I prefer to conceal the hook completely, especially when fishing clear water in bright sunlight. Dace, in particular, will sometimes neatly nip off the bottom of the caster, leaving intact that part which contains the hook. If the hook is completely hidden inside the caster, they will be less likely to indulge in this annoying habit. Some fish may be missed, but at least the bites do develop to a stage where they can be hit with reasonable chances of success.

There has been much speculation among anglers as to why

casters often produce a better class of fish than maggots. I think there are several reasons. One is that the caster sinks at a faster rate than the small maggot and is thus more likely to be taken by the larger fish, which usually lie nearer to the bottom. The caster is also normally fished without fine groundbait, which often attracts hordes of small fish and increases the competition for food. It is completely different from the maggot and from the tiny organisms upon which small fish feed, too; and this fact probably contributes a great deal towards its tendency to sort out the bigger fish from the small ones.

Since most anglers only use casters, the question of choice between floaters and sinkers as a bait is not likely to arise. Yet it is obviously a matter of some importance since surface-feeding fish are more likely to succumb to a surface-fished chrysalid than to one fished beneath the surface. The reverse is equally true, of course. If the fish are rising or can be seen near to the surface, I choose a floater. If not, a sinker would be the logical choice. Floaters are generally much more effective during the summer and autumn, when both roach and dace fall readily to them. No canal angler can really afford to be without these two forms of chrysalid bait.

Bread-flake

No canal angler should neglect this bait. It is cheap, easy to obtain and clean; and most species of fish will accept it. Some anglers use little else and have brought the fishing of bread-flake 'on the drop' to a fine art. In my opinion, bread in all its forms is one of the most useful baits available. I use it often – particularly during the winter months, when it is especially deadly for roach.

No preparation is necessary. A new unsliced loaf is all that is needed. Flake is torn roughly from the inside of the loaf and squeezed gently around the shank of the hook. The size of the flake depends largely upon the type of fish being sought. Very small fragments, fished on size 14 or 16 hooks, might be called for when small to medium roach are the quarry; but for the larger fish, both the size of the hook and the bait can be increased proportionately. I often use thumbnail-sized pieces on hooks of up to size 6 for big roach, and even larger than this when chub are the quarry.

Stale loaves are useless for successful flake fishing. The loaf should be new and moist. Flake from a new loaf will stay on the hook better, and is equally effective when fished either in a slow-sinking style or hard on the bottom. Tradition favours slow-sinking for roach; but no angler should restrict his fishing to this style.

Crust

Crust is another excellent bait for big roach, dace and chub. It is tougher and more buoyant than flake and, for this reason, some anglers soak it before using it. I have never found it necessary to take such a step. I use mine as I use flake – torn straight from the sides and the bottom of the loaf. The darker, crisper crust from the top of the loaf is not usually as effective a lure.

I find crust most deadly when fished on the bottom – where, because of its greater buoyancy, it remains visible even when fished on a bed of reed. More weight is needed to sink this bait: but if it is carefully balanced against the size of the crust, there is no need to sacrifice anything in the way of delicacy and lightness of presentation. A crust bait, properly weighted, will sink just as slowly as a more lightly weighted flake bait. It can also be fished on the surface on a weightless line to take such fish as chub, dace and roach, too, when they are rising.

The size of the bait can vary from a tiny fragment fished on a size 12 hook to a piece the size of a matchbox, fished on hooks of up to size 2 when chub are the quarry. Chub have large mouths and can take a bait of this size with ease.

Bread-paste

This bait is not as widely used by canal anglers as it once was, probably because of the present vogue for maggot and caster fishing. Baits that are out of fashion often tend to be under-rated, though. Paste was a favourite bait a decade ago, and there is no logical reason why it should not be as effective now as it was then. Though it lacks the light, absorbent qualities that make flake such a deadly bait for the slow-sinking style, soft white paste can be equally deadly for both roach and chub.

It should not be used when the bottom is composed of soft mud or where there is a thick growth of bottom reed. Flake or crust is better. Paste, being heavier, tends to sink into the debris and become hidden. It is most effective when fished on a bottom of clean gravel or in the faster water below the lock gates. There is no reason why it should not be fished in the slow-sinking style too, especially where there is a strong current to counteract the greater weight of the paste. Another advantage of paste over flake is that it will stay on the hook longer, so dispensing with the need for continual rebaiting.

The most important aspect of bread-paste as a bait concerns its preparation. It should never be made from a new loaf, but from the crumbly interior of a stale one. This should be soaked and then carefully pressed in a damp rag until it attains a soft, clinging consistency. It should not be hard, dry or lumpy. If it is, it might stay on the hook longer – but it will lure less fish.

Like flake, paste can be used in varying sizes. A small portion, fished on a size 12 or 14 hook, is normal for roach. Larger portions should be fished on larger hooks: sizes from 10 to 4, even. I have caught many roach and gudgeon on pinpoint pieces of paste, and plenty of big roach, chub and some bream on larger pieces of paste fished on big hooks. Even pike will sometimes pick up a large piece of paste.

Cheese

This is another fine but neglected bait. Some great roach can be caught with it, and it has also accounted for several specimen chub in recent years.

As with bread-paste, the consistency of cheese bait is all important. If it is too hard, it will be rejected. Really soft cheese can be used neat. Cheese that has gone hard should be grated and blended with stale bread to form a soft paste. It may fly off the hook if the cast is made sharply; but that can be avoided by making the cast in a gentle, underhanded swinging style rather than in the overhead style that is favoured by many canal anglers. If a long rod is used, it is also possible to reach out and virtually lower the bait into the swim. The risk of the bait flying off the hook is thus eliminated.

The type and colour of the cheese is not too important. I favour a strong-flavoured cheese like mature Cheddar or Lancashire. I also prefer red cheese to white, but I cannot advance any logical reason for this preference. At the moment, no positive proof exists that fish prefer red cheese to white. Gorgonzola is sometimes very killing but it usually takes time to get the roach and chub feeding on this bait, especially if it has been little-used in the canal. This probably explains why it is not a popular bait with match anglers. Experience reveals that it is a better bait for summer use than winter. July and August seem to be the peak months in my canals.

Worms

Worms are among the best all-round baits available but, again, are strangely neglected by the majority of canal anglers. Perch love them. So do tench and chub. Both eels and pike will take them; and contrary to popular opinion, some fine roach can be caught with them too. To complete the list, there are few better baits for chub than a big lobworm.

Many different species of worm exist. The canal angler need only concern himself with two kinds: the lobworm and the red worm. Lobworms are most easily found on lawns, tennis-courts, bowling-greens and cricket-pitches at night, when there is some dew on the grass. The period immediately following a heavy rainfall is most productive. I have gathered them in hundreds at such times.

Some anglers use the tail only for roach fishing, but I often use the whole worm and have caught many fine roach, as well as perch and chub. A larger hook than is generally used is advisable. I regard size 10 as the absolute minimum. A size 8 or 6 is better, especially when chub or tench is the quarry.

Red worms are another fine bait. When used in quantity and fished on a smaller hook than that used for lobworms, they will lure tench, perch, bream, chub and roach. The best places to find them are in rotted-down compost or manure heaps, beneath old sacking and rotted wood, and almost anywhere where the ground is soft and damp. An old disused manure heap is usually a prolific breeding ground for them. The only drawback with these worms is that they are also attractive to minnows. Wherever these nuisance fish can be found in quantity, the lobworm will probably prove the better of the two baits.

SEED-BAITS

Malt

If there is one bait the seeker of good canal roach cannot afford to overlook, it is this one. Yet it is strangely neglected, maggots or bread being preferred by the vast majority of canal anglers. This is difficult to understand when one considers what a fine bait malt is for roach. It would be tedious to list all the excellent catches of roach I have had with this bait; but I can recall one catch consisting of no less than a hundred and twenty-five fish, and many others where I counted the fish caught in scores. Any bait that can lure roach in such quantities must obviously be given serious consideration.

Malt is not a new bait. It was known and used as far back as the seventeenth century, at least. Walton's *Compleat Angler* contains a specific reference to it. 'Take a handful of well-made malt, free from husks; put a small quantity of fresh water to it, and set it in something that is fit for that purpose over the fire, where it should boil leisurely and softly,' he wrote when referring to the preparation of this bait. As he said, malt should be boiled slowly – and preferably after soaking overnight. He knew all about its effectiveness as a bait, too: 'If your hook be small and good, you will find this to be a very choice bait.'

When cooked, the grains of malt should be nearly twice their original size, and they should have a firm white centre. Overcooking will cause the malt to fragment and become too soft to use on the hook. An alternative method of cooking is to prepare the malt in a vacuum flask. Personally, I prefer to cook mine in a saucepan. A greater quantity can be prepared, and it is also possible to keep a close watch on the malt so that it does not get spoiled.

An important point to remember when using malt, or any other seed-bait, is that it sinks quickly and does not disintegrate. This means that it will not only attract fish but will also feed them. It is therefore important not to overfeed the swim with the grains. A handful or so to attract the fish and then a few grains at intervals is a wise tactic once the roach are feeding on it. A useful groundbait that disperses in the water can be made from crushed malt. This tends to attract the smaller fish, and it is a useful aid when quick results are desirable. But I prefer to use the grains whole and fish without groundbait. I find I catch more good fish that way.

A feature of malt fishing that is worth noting is that it is generally far more effective during the warm summer months than in the winter. It is also more selective than most baits since minnows and other small fish are less inclined to take it than they are maggots or bread-flake. It will also produce far more roach than other fish, although both chub and bream like it.

Wheat

Closely allied to malt in appearance and effectiveness, wheat is another neglected bait that is deadly for several species. Roach love it; chub can soon acquire a taste for it; and both tench and bream can sometimes be caught with it. Like malt, it should be stewed slowly. The best results are obtained by pre-soaking and then cooking until the grains are well swollen and showing a firm white centre. Wheat tends to swell more than malt. If overcooked, it splits completely. This does not seem to detract from its effectiveness, though, provided that it has not been allowed to become too soft. It should not be left in the water when cooking is completed, but it should be drained and put into a cloth bag or tin. I like to use mine fresh. In warm weather like malt, it soon goes sour and is then less attractive. For this reason, it is best to cook only a limited amount at any one time. For best results, it should be fished on a size 12 or 14 hook; double grains on a size 10. Big roach and chub are sometimes not averse to double grains.

I usually start using wheat around July. Tradition has it that it should be used at harvest time, when the grain is being cut in the fields. I have never understood why. In its natural state, wheat is hard and unpalatable. Any wheat that found its way into the water would be uneatable. I use it throughout the summer – sometimes right up until the beginning of November, if the weather remains mild.

Hemp

This is probably the best known of all the seed-baits, and it needs little introduction to most anglers. It is especially deadly for roach, but chub and dace will take it too if it is persisted with. Hemp can be boiled more quickly than the other baits. Cooking should be terminated as soon as the white

37

shoot appears. Overcooking will lead to the grains splitting open completely, and they will then be unusable.

Hemp is not as easy to obtain as it once was, and it has become much more expensive. It must also be fished on a very small hook: size 16 or 18, usually. For these reasons, I tend not to use it as much as I once did. I prefer the more easily obtained wheat and malt – and there is no reason to suppose that roach prefer hemp to the other seed-baits. I use all three in my local canal, and it has been my experience that none of them is habit-forming. Roach do not become addicted to them. A feeding pattern can be established with any of them if they are persisted with long enough. That same pattern can be broken by switching from one to the other. I have proved this many times. It takes time and patience, but it can be done. The banning of hemp, or any other seed-bait, on the grounds that it drugs the fish or makes them impossible to catch with any other bait, seems to me to be nonsense.

The other myth about hemp fishing – that it is always necessary to strike quickly to hit the lightning-swift bites one is supposed to get – is also a fallacy. If the hemp is fished on the bottom and the tackle is correctly adjusted, the bites are usually no swifter than those one gets when using other seed-baits. The difficulty that is sometimes experienced in the actual hooking of roach is probably due more to the smallness of the hook used and also to the fact that roach sometimes pull at the weights or brush the line in passing, thus giving false indications of bites.

Hemp is an excellent bait but inferior, in my opinion, to malt or wheat.

Other Baits

There are other baits that can be used, such as macaroni, pearl-barley, rice and maize; and some 'natural' baits such as shrimps, woodlice, live flies and other insects. But the baits I have listed should be sufficient to enable any canal angler to fish the season through with confidence.

Other lures, such as flies, live-baits and spinners, have only a limited and more specialized use. With the exception of the live-baits, they do not properly fall into the category of baits normally used by the average canal angler. These are dealt with later. Meanwhile, there are the more important matters of method, style and presentation to be considered.

A full understanding of the many different ways of catching fish is essential to those who wish to get the best out of their canal fishing. One bait and one method might sometimes suffice; but the angler who knows how and when to ring the changes with his baits and methods will catch far more fish and probably enjoy his fishing far more, too.

CHAPTER 4

Groundbaiting

Fine groundbait – or 'cloudbait', as it is sometimes called – is regarded as indispensable by the majority of canal anglers. Few would go fishing without it. The amount dumped into any hard-fished canal during a match or in the course of a normal summer weekend must be astronomical. It is of some significance that the amount of good fish caught does not seem to justify the faith most anglers display in this item. I use it very little. I believe that, in certain circumstances, the thoughtless use of this kind of groundbait can have a detrimental effect on the angler's chances. On the other hand, there are times and occasions when groundbait, properly used, can result in far more fish being caught than would otherwise have been caught.

I think the cardinal sin is to use groundbait merely from force of habit, without regard to the circumstances or the species of fish being sought. Not all days are alike. Not all waters are alike. And not all fish are alike. Conditions change and circumstances change. The successful angler does nothing blindly. He must have a reason. Usually, he has a specific aim in mind. And if that aim can be best achieved by using groundbait, he will use it. If not, he will put it aside. But the indiscriminate user does not think deeply enough. He arrives at his swim, tackles up his rod and throws his groundbait in as a matter of course. If he does not catch fish, he will not usually concede that the fault could be his. It is the fault of the water, the conditions or the fish.

The fact is that groundbait does not guarantee success. Indeed, it is often possible to catch fish without using groundbait at all. A ball of groundbait thrown into a swim can make a noise equivalent to that made by a stone. Sound travels quickly through water. Fish are very sensitive to sound. It is also probable that, in many cases, the appearance of the angler over the swim has a scaring effect. It seems logical, then, to assume that the angler who habitually indulges in this kind of behaviour must often scare more fish than he ever suspects; and that his thoughtlessness quite often condemns him to failure, or to a long period of fruitless waiting which he need not have endured.

Contrast this approach with the approach of the angler who has learned that there are times when his purpose will be best served by casting the bait into the swim without any preliminary groundbaiting at all. He will have his rod tackled up ready and his bait on the hook before he gets to his chosen swim. He will keep low and take advantage of any cover that is available to him. It is then quite possible that the bait will be taken by a fish already in the swim. The fish sees the bait falling slowly and naturally down through the water and moves quickly to intercept it. What is more natural? Surprisingly, though, many anglers are not prepared to believe that fish can be caught from a canal in this manner. Tradition and prejudice die hard. It takes time, experience and effort to dispel the attitudes of a lifetime. Most prefer to stick to a well-tried routine; and it is left to a few individuals to prove that nothing is certain in angling, nothing can be taken for granted. To fish without groundbait seems an imposition, a handicap – until the angler has tried it and found that groundbait is not indispensable after all.

Of course, quick captures made without the use of groundbait cannot be guaranteed. In the natural course of events, it is quite probable that the ratio of success will be low. But at least the angler who fishes like this demonstrates that he understands that fish can sometimes be caught quickly without groundbait. He is fishing thoughtfully, with intent. If his first attempt fails, then he will begin to think seriously about using groundbait to attract the kind of fish he wants. It will not necessarily be the fine cloudbait variety, though.

Cloudbait has its uses, of course. If it is the angler's aim merely to catch fish, irrespective of size and species, then it is likely that his interests will be best served by careful groundbaiting with slow-sinking particles of crushed bread mixed, perhaps, with quantities of pinkies – the small maggots that sink slowly and attractively down through the swim. His bait, carefully impaled on the tiny sharp hook, will sink through the swim at approximately the same rate of descent as the groundbait. This is the traditional style of the canal angler – in some cases a style as undeviating and ritualistic as any religious ceremony. It succeeds often enough to give its habitual users a sound basis of argument for its perpetuation.

Sometimes many fish are attracted by this kind of groundbait, particularly small fish. It is designed to attract them at a level where they are most numerous and active – between surface and mid-water. The cloud of groundbait hangs in the swim while the maggots sink slowly, twisting and turning in the near-still water, vulnerable to attack. The small fish are greedy and not easily scared. Large quantities of them are sometimes caught by anglers skilled in the art of fishing a tiny bait on fine tackle. The anglers expect results and fish in a manner calculated to get those results.

The real test of an angler's ability comes when his tried and trusted methods fail. He may try hurling more groundbait into the swim to 'bring the fish on', as anglers say. But it is not certain that such a tactic will bring about a dramatic change in his fortunes. The fish may be sated with food. Or they might have been scared off by a pike, or by the angler himself. If so, perhaps it would be better for him to move off and try a different pitch with different tactics.

There are many pitfalls connected with groundbaiting. It is so easy to make a mistake; easier still to blame the water or the fish when an established ritual fails. A clear understanding of what the function of groundbaiting is, why we use it and what form it should take if we do use it is necessary at this stage.

Basically, groundbait is used to attract fish, to concentrate them into a specific area, and to start them feeding. Many anglers feel that it should attract but not feed – the underlying idea being that the fish will accept the hook-bait more readily if the groundbait only attracts. The composition of this kind of groundbait varies, but its purpose – that of attracting the fish but not feeding them – remains basically unchanged. Proprietary brands can be bought, but some anglers prefer to make up their own. Bread, dried and crushed into fine particles, forms an excellent base for all fine groundbaits. It can be made heavier and more solid by mixing in sausage-rusk or wheatmeal. Some anglers include dried milk powder, or soak the mixture in milk. This blend produces a groundbait that sinks slowly and, at the same time, emits a milky cloud which hangs in the water and is slowly carried away downstream.

I have tried this mixture many times and can vouch for its effectiveness. Its attractive slow-sinking properties can be increased by blending scraps of bread-flake. In the normal course of events, this kind of groundbait will attract hordes of small fish, and perhaps some larger ones too.

There are no absolute certainties in angling. One cannot say that this kind of groundbaiting will *not* lure big fish, because it can and sometimes does. What is certain is that more small fish will be caught than large ones, and that the majority of these will be small roach. All my experience indicates that the angler seeking a better class of fish needs a different approach – a different groundbait altogether, if he is going to use one at all. There are many more small fish than large ones in canals. The angler seeking larger fish must study and think how best he can avoid the small ones.

He might, as I have suggested, refrain from using ground-bait at all until he has explored the chances of an immediate capture. Then, and only then, will he begin to think about using groundbait. It is not likely, though, that he will use the slow-sinking variety or anything like it. There is a reason for this. The smaller fish is intent on gleaning tiny particles of food. It is not yet ready for the larger items. The bigger roach, rudd, tench and bream have passed through this stage. True, they may still eat microscopic foods, but the larger items are more attractive to them now – nymphs, live insects, molluscs and the food the angler deposits in the canal for them. Such food is more plentiful in the lower stratas of water, and the competition from hordes of small fish is less intense. Quite often the larger fish, especially the bream, will feed directly off the bottom and will seldom seek food in the stratas of water inhabited by fish in the early stages of their growth.

The implications of this, as far as the angler is concerned, are obvious. If he does not want to attract small fish, he will choose a quicker-sinking groundbait; and it will contain items of food upon which the bigger fish can feed. The fine cloud-bait, so beloved by canal anglers, will be put aside. His groundbait will closely resemble the hook-bait he intends to use. It may even consist entirely of the hook-bait.

If, for instance, he intends to fish with flake, it is likely that his groundbait will consist entirely of soaked flake. The new loaf, which is not normally used for groundbaiting, will prob-ably be preferred to the stale loaf which produces fine par-ticles. When soaked in milk, the new loaf emits a white cloud which lingers in the swim while the heavier flakes sink slowly to the bottom. In canals where the current is negligible, this type of groundbait will not travel far from the spot where it is thrown in. If the current is medium to strong, it will be carried some distance downstream – and this fact must be borne in mind when throwing it in. In those places where the current is strong, much heavier groundbait must be used. Paste is a good substitute. It can be tossed into the swim in portions roughly the size of a fingernail. The same procedure should be followed with cheese and with crust. The latter is extremely buoyant and needs soaking thoroughly, otherwise it will float and be useless as a groundbait.

The use of such groundbait might seem strange to many canal anglers. It appears to be the antithesis of all that is considered normal for canal fishing. This may be so; but I can assure sceptics that these tactics do produce results. One of the largest catches of big canal roach that I have ever taken followed persistent groundbaiting with soaked new bread. At one stage, I was netting pound-plus roach almost every swim-down; and I could quote many other instances when this kind of groundbaiting has helped me to catch fine roach of a far bigger average size than those usually caught. The same is true of the paste groundbait and the cheese. Both sink quickly. Both are far less attractive to small fish than the traditional groundbait. They do not guarantee success, of course, but they do ensure that the angler is fishing with more than an even chance that the fish he catches will be above average size.

Groundbaiting with one or other of the seed-baits is another tactic which will often yield better than average fish, especially roach. Seed-baits sink quickly and are not as attractive to small fish as other groundbaits. If a finer variety of groundbait is required, seed-baits can be crushed and mixed with bread or meal. This will give a mixture that sinks at a slower rate than the seeds. I use such mixtures rarely. The best results, in my experience, are obtained by feeding the swim with loose grains – a quantity at first; then a few grains at intervals. Again, groundbait of this type bears little resemblance to the traditional kind, but it can be extremely effective. I use it frequently during the summer months, and have caught many fine nets of roach, some chub and even bream after groundbaiting with it. Minnows are attracted to the seeds; so are small roach. But it is not easy for them to pick up this bait before it reaches the bottom. The number of small fish caught after groundbaiting with seed-baits is therefore very small when compared with the numbers caught when groundbaiting with fine cloudbait.

Big maggots, used alone, form an effective groundbait. They sink more quickly than the smaller maggots, and thus become more attractive and more vulnerable to the larger fish. Worms are similarly attractive. There are few better groundbaits than broken worms for big roach, perch and chub. I have taken many fine nets of canal roach after groundbaiting with worms. The attractiveness of worm groundbait lies almost certainly in its odour and, to a lesser extent, in its appearance of life. By comparison, groundbaits composed of bread are less attractive. Albert Oldfield – that renowned angler whose exploits on his home water, the Macclesfield Canal, are well known – is a firm believer in the attractiveness of worms as a groundbait for big canal roach.

It should now be obvious that the type of groundbait used is of great importance. Generally speaking, if quick results with small fish are wanted, the angler's purpose will be best served by using the traditional kind of fine cloudbait. But if better-quality fish are wanted, some deviation from this practice is more likely to yield the desired result. This is only an opinion. But it is an opinion based on a lot of practical experience, and it is worth considering. Meanwhile, several other important aspects of groundbaiting must be examined: the amount used; the rate at which it should be used; and when it should be used to get the best results.

Match anglers use large quantities of groundbait, but theirs is a specialized form of canal fishing. We are concerned with the tactics of the individual angler who is not involved in competition but just wants to catch fish. The question of how much groundbait he will need is not as vital to him as to the match angler, but it is important to a degree. A wrong decision can ruin his chances; a right one can enhance them considerably.

Canals are not like rivers, which usually have well-defined swims of varying character. Canals are uniform; they have little or no current. This means that the groundbait will not travel far from the point at which it is thrown in but will gradually sink and remain on the bottom. Its function as an attraction for fish which might be lying a long way downstream is therefore limited. So the canal angler will normally require far less groundbait than the angler fishing a big, wide river. The rate at which he introduces his groundbait will depend largely upon the numbers of fish that are in his swim, and also upon how quickly they respond.

In this sense, he is working in the dark. Unless he can actually see the fish, he has no means of knowing how many there are or what species they are. He must fish and find out. It could be that he will need very little groundbait. There are times when canal fish need no artificial encouragement to feed. If groundbait is needed, it is likely that a little thrown in at intervals will suit his purpose best. It is not wise to dump it all in at once. Such action will almost certainly mean that he will catch less fish than he would otherwise have caught.

The part played by groundbait as a stimulant must not be forgotten, either. If fish see a bait often enough, it is most likely that they will eventually begin to feed upon it. Fish – especially shoal fish – are largely creatures of habit and instinct. What one does, the others will often do too. This can mean intense competition for available food. The maxim of 'little and often' with the groundbait will ensure that the shoal will stay in or near the swim and keep feeding for as long as they are hungry.

This kind of groundbaiting is closely geared to the idea of extracting the maximum number of fish in the shortest possible time. In this sense, it has a special connexion with match fishing. The aims of the specimen hunter and the seeker of better-class fish are best served by prebaiting the swim with samples of the hook-bait rather than with fine groundbait, which does not provide sufficient feed to keep the big fish interested and may also attract far too many small fish. This is the last thing the big-fish hunter wants. His aim must be to eliminate such competition as far as he is able.

Some anglers doubt that there is any advantage to be gained from prebaiting a swim. I disagree. My experiences indicate that there are great advantages to be gained from prebaiting. Consider, for instance, what the odds are against a casually fished bait being found by the bigger fish – bearing in mind the amount of water it has to move around in and the vast number of other fish that are always in direct competition for food. Obviously, any action which will help to draw the bigger fish into a more confined and accessible area must be worth considering. Prebaiting does not guarantee that such a desirable state of affairs will result, but it can help to lessen the odds considerably.

Obviously, fine groundbait composed of bread crumbs and

similar mixtures will be of limited use in any campaign of prebaiting. Since the aim is to draw the better-class fish into a specific area and start them feeding confidently on the chosen hook-bait, the groundbait must consist mostly, if not entirely, of the hook-bait. A heavy groundbait composed of bread-flake or paste is desirable if one is going to use bread baits. A liberal supply of worms should be used if the intention is to fish with worms. There is virtually no limit to the type of bait that can be used. The amount used, and the duration of the prebaiting period, must be governed largely by the time needed to start the fish feeding on the chosen bait.

In the case of worms, it is not likely that a prolonged campaign of prebaiting will be necessary. Neither will it with bread or cheese, in most waters. It is when one uses the more unusual baits, such as the seed-baits, that a longer period of prebaiting might be necessary. If the bait has not been used in the water before, several days of patient prebaiting might be necessary before any worthwhile results are obtained.

In some instances, however, a single act of prebaiting might suffice. Each water is different, and one cannot say with certainty how long it will take to get fish feeding on a new bait. My own experience indicates a variation from a few hours to several days. The fish caught – which are mostly roach but might also include chub, bream, or tench, depending upon the type of groundbait used – are usually better than average size, if fewer in number. Seed-baits tend to produce a preponderance of roach. Lobworms also produce roach, but quite possibly perch or tench too. Bread-baits rule out perch but can result in a concentration of any one of the other species mentioned. Much depends upon the number of each species in the canal and also the swim chosen.

Possibly the greatest advantage that results from prebaiting is the fact that the angler can go to his chosen swim with a great deal more confidence than if he were fishing it for the very first time without prebaiting. Now he has reason to hope that there might be several good fish in his swim. All he has to do is approach the swim quietly and toss in his hook-bait. It might be taken at once. I have done this more times than I can remember, and very rarely are the fish caught in this manner of small size.

CHAPTER 5

Clear-water Roach Fishing

The roach-fishing style for canals is traditionally fine, far off and, usually, slow sinking. This style cannot always be used, but it occupies an important position in the canal angler's repertoire. It is frequently used in clear waters, and there is nothing difficult about it. Basically, the bait is fished on a weightless or very lightly weighted line with the object of tempting the roach to accept the bait as it is falling slowly down through the water.

This style of fishing can be a deadly method for roach, especially for the smaller fish. Lines with a breaking strain as low as three-quarters of a pound are sometimes used in conjunction with the tiniest of floats and hooks to achieve the most natural action possible in the presentation of the bait. The float is usually attached to the line by two rubber bands: one at the bottom of the float; the other close to its tip (Fig 6).

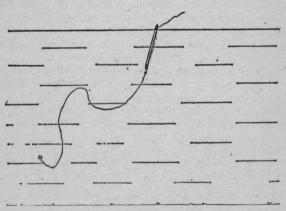

Figure 6. Tackle for fishing slow-sinking bait using both rings

At first, it might seem difficult to cast such fine tackle any distance; but it is surprising how easy it really is when used in conjunction with a well-filled spool of fine line and a long, supple rod. I usually experience little difficulty in casting a small quill clear across a canal – unless there is a brisk inshore breeze, which complicates presentation. But this can be overcome by using a small self-cocking float.

This type of float, which is usually made from pith or balsa wood, has the necessary weight embodied in the float itself. This means that weight attached to the cast can be reduced to a minimum or, in some circumstances, dispensed with altogether. Casting across the canal is easy with this type of float. A flick of the wrist is all that is needed.

The one fault with this float is the tendency of the line to curl over the tip of the float while it is airborne. This happens because the float, being relatively heavy, travels through the air at a much faster rate than the terminal tackle. The defect can be minimized by using a long rod to lower the bait into the water, or by placing the top rubber band as close to the tip of the float as possible and slowing down the entry of the float into the water when the limit of the cast is reached. This is done by letting the line run through the fingers – usually over the forefinger. It also helps to have a shot close to the hook.

Sometimes it might be necessary to add more weight, especially if flake or crust is being used as bait. Both of these baits contain air and are therefore more buoyant than, say, one of the seed-baits. Naturally, they take longer to sink. Therefore, unless the roach are actually rising to take food from the surface, additional weight is necessary to carry the bait slowly down through the swim. The amount of weight needed will vary according to the size of the bait. For a small piece of flake, a single dust shot would probably suffice. Crust would need more weight – probably a No 6 shot. The important thing is to maintain the slow-sinking style. The bait must not lie on the surface, but neither must it plummet quickly to the bottom. Both bait and weight must be carefully matched if the method is to function properly.

A slight variation on this style of fishing can be achieved by attaching the float by threading the line twice through the bottom ring. This style is often used to combat drift, and it is said to increase striking efficiency. But I do not care for this method. It leaves kinks in the line and increases the risk of breakage through weakening caused by friction, especially if the float is moved up and down the line without first being loosened where it is threaded through the float ring.

A better way is to thread the line once through the bottom ring and then through a rubber band situated just above the ring. A small shot can then be carefully attached to the line, below the ring, to prevent any slipping that might occur when striking. A variation on the same style can be achieved by attaching two shots close to the float – one below the bottom ring; the other just above it. This, I believe, gives cleaner, better striking action while still retaining the basic slow-sinking effect. It is particularly useful when using a larger float since the weight can be concentrated in the two shots, which are attached close to the float ring. Figure 7 illustrates both rings. I wrote of this method in an article which appeared in *Angling Times* dated February 14th, 1958. It is now quite a popular method.

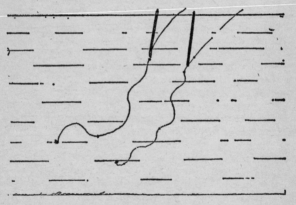

Figure 7. Two methods of slow-sinking style using bottom ring only

Another method I often use is to thread the float once through the bottom ring, and then tie on two rubber stops – one below the float and the other above it, at the depth to which the bait is to be allowed to fall. One shot, which should be sufficient to sink the bait, should then be attached midway between the bottom stop and the hook, with a dust shot squeezed on closer to the hook for better bite registration (Fig 8). The float rests against the bottom stop before casting; but as soon as it alights in the water, it slides up the line until it reaches the limit imposed by the upper stop. At this point, it should settle and cock in the water. If the float sticks, it can usually be freed by a gentle jerking of the rod-tip. I have caught some grand nets of roach while using this method in calm clear-water conditions. It allows the bait to sink in a most natural manner and also increases striking efficiency, since the line runs freely through the float ring.

A float with two rings – one situated close to the tip of the

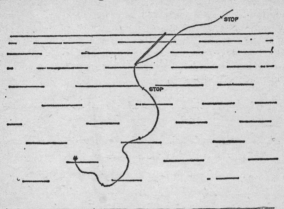

Figure 8. Slow-sinking style using running float with two stops

float and the other at the bottom – can be used if preferred. This type of float, which is a recognizable type of 'slider', can be bought. It can also be made easily enough. Since it is less likely to stick than the other type, it is more popular.

Another variation on the same style is what I call a 'tube float'. This is fashioned from a thin plastic tube which is passed through a cork body. In appearance it is very much like an antenna float. The line is threaded through the centre tube, and the stops and weight are attached to the line as before. Its disadvantage is that it is more susceptible to drift, and therefore should not be used in breezy conditions. It functions best in the conditions of flat calm (Fig 9).

It can now be seen that there are several excellent ways of presenting a bait in a slow-sinking style. The final choice of tackle is often dictated as much by personal preference as by any other reason. Differences of opinion must be expected, but they are not really important as long as the basic aim of achieving a deceptive presentation of the bait is achieved. What I feel to be more important than personal preference in the matter of tackle is that it should be clearly understood that this style is not a static kind of fishing calling for patience and fortitude. Indeed, the angler who is content to cast his bait in and leave it will probably catch substantially fewer fish than the angler who is prepared to work for his fish by continually casting and re-casting to take fish 'on the drop'. Once the bait has reached maximum fall, it may have passed through the feeding area and thus become less likely to be taken. It is

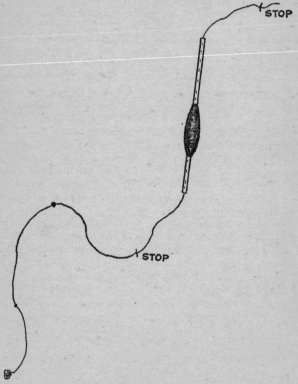

Figure 9. Hollow tube 'slider' with two stops

obviously bad tactics to leave it there. Instead, it should be retrieved and cast again. The angler must be prepared to work for his fish if he wishes to catch the maximum number in the shortest possible time.

This is particularly so when small roach are the quarry. They tend to move about in large shoals and to take their feed most freely in the higher stratas of water. The finest of tackle and the most delicately adjusted float are advisable to catch such fish. I once watched an angler take a mixed catch of eighty-five small roach and gudgeon while fishing a slow-sinking bait across the canal. His line was one pound breaking strain; hook, size 20; float, a tiny quill. The tackle was weighted with one dust shot, placed about two inches from the hook. The idea was to pick up roach 'on the drop' and then gudgeon off the bottom if the bait was not taken while it was sinking. By concentrating the fish into a small area close to the reeds opposite him with some accurate groundbaiting and casting, he was able to build up this impressive catch of fish in a very short time indeed.

It is questionable, of course, whether so much effort and trouble was worth while in view of the size of the fish caught – none of which exceeded five inches in length. I think it was, because the angler was a match angler and he was getting in some valuable match experience on this water. In a sense, you could say he got the best of both worlds: fish off the top and off the bottom. Had there been no gudgeon in his swim he would, no doubt, have adjusted his style to take roach only by reducing the depth at which the bait was being fished when it reached maximum fall.

It is also worth noting that on this same day, and in the same canal, I was using a totally different style and different bait and was catching a much different class of roach. My bait was malt, fished on a bottom of clean gravel in around four feet of water. I used no groundbait; only a few grains of the malt, tossed into the swim at intervals. Bites developed slowly; but I caught thirty-five roach – the smallest weighing six ounces, the largest weighing just over a pound. On this occasion, I made no attempt to fish across the canal, under the far bank. Instead, I fished the boat-track about ten yards downstream of my position on the bank. The water was very clear and there was very little wind; but as there were no other anglers present, I felt that I had a good chance of contacting roach at closer range. The style of fishing I used was what I call the 'flat-float' method. This is a bottom-fishing style which often pays dividends when the water is very calm (Fig 10).

It is very simple to rig up. One small shot is attached to the line a few inches from the hook, and the float is set at a depth in excess of the depth of the water. The float, which is attached by both rings, lies flat when it is first cast into the water; and it will continue to lie flat until the surface drift tightens up the slack line and causes it to cock slightly. When the roach picks up the bait, the float will again lie flat – and the strike should be made immediately.

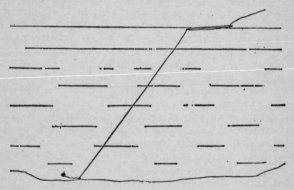

Figure 10. Flat-float method

I used this method in preference to the slow-sinking style mainly because, in my experience, a better class of roach can often be caught with a seed-bait fished on the bottom. It is altogether a slower, lazier style of fishing; but it does produce results once the roach begin to feed, providing the bottom is clean. Had there been a thick carpet of silkweed in the swim, I would have used a different style entirely.

Another very sensitive method of bottom fishing in calm conditions is the 'lift' method, so called because the float rises up in the water when a fish picks up the bait. This method, like most good methods, is basically simple. The idea is that the *combined* weight of the shot and bait should just sink the float.

Let us suppose that we have decided to use a maggot or one of the seed-baits. A shot is then chosen that will just sink the bait when the hook is baited. This shot is squeezed on to the line about an inch from the hook, and it must rest on the bottom. The float, which is attached to the line by a thick rubber band at the bottom end only, should sink slowly beneath the water. The depth can then be adjusted so that the float just shows above the surface. Peacock quills are favourites for this method because they can be cut in sizes to suit the weight chosen; but other floats, including the antenna type, can also be used. The instructions for arranging the tackle must be rigidly adhered to, otherwise the method will not function satisfactorily. Ideally, the float should rise, or 'lift', in the water, giving a clear indication of a bite when a roach picks up the bait.

In practice, it does not matter if the float is submerged slightly – provided that its exact position is known – since it will rise like a periscope as soon as a bite develops. In very clear water, it is possible to see the float easily enough even when it is submerged, so there is no loss of efficiency.

A defect becomes obvious, however, once the surface of the water is broken up by a breeze. If the float is beneath the surface, it cannot now be seen. On the other hand, if it is exposed to view – and to the wind – by sliding it up the line slightly, it will probably be blown out of position. The solution is to use an antenna float with a very thin spine tip, weighted as before so that at least two-thirds of the spine is submerged and the remaining third is visible. The effect of wind on this type of float is slight; and when a roach picks up the bait, the float will lift in the normal way. It helps to paint the tip with alternating stripes of contrasting colours, such as black and white. Bites are then even easier to detect (Fig 11).

One item of equipment that must not be forgotten when using this method is a rod-rest. Without a rest in which to place the rod, it is not possible to hold the float steady enough to retain the sensitivity to the tiniest bite that is its greatest asset. It is also advisable to use the method as close to the rod-tip as possible. The less line exposed to the elements the better. A long rod, though not essential, is definitely a great advantage.

The long rod is clearly even more valuable when fishing the far bank, especially if it is desirable to hold the float there in troublesome wind conditions. The most important thing is to overcome the surface drift of the water as far as possible. This is done by sinking the line slightly. Very fine monofilaments have good floating properties, so it is best to rub the line lightly with a cloth soaked in detergent to remove excess grease. A dust shot, gently squeezed on to the line above the

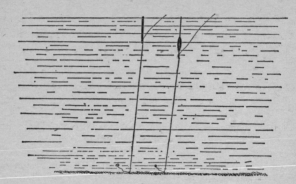

Figure 11. 'Lift' method using peacock quill and antenna float

float, also helps to sink the line; but care must be exercised when doing this or the line may be seriously weakened. I have experimented with a small swivel, which runs freely along the line above the float and does not weaken the line in any way. This is preferable to the split shot, in my opinion; but it must, of course, be threaded on to the line before the float. A small

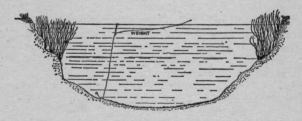

Figure 12. Fishing the far bank with sunken line

rubber stop, tied on to the line above the float, will prevent it from sliding down and remaining hard up against the float (Fig 12). A tiny piece of lead foil can also be used to sink the line.

When using this style, the shotting must be adjusted so that the bait will be fished where it is going to be most effective. If it is required to sink to the bottom, the shot should be close to the hook and the depth must be carefully adjusted so that the bait will reach bottom at maximum fall. To fish the bait off-bottom, the depth must be altered so that the bait will not fall to the bottom. But the basic set-up remains otherwise un-altered. This is a very sensitive method of bottom fishing for roach in those parts of the canal where the current is negligible.

Whatever method is used, some thought should be given to the arrangement of the tackle. It is not always sufficient merely to fish the bait on the bottom. It must be fished in such a manner that the roach can pick it up without feeling the drag of the float or weight. This is not difficult to achieve when fishing a slow-sinking bait; but the matter becomes a little more complex when bottom fishing – especially where there is a strong current – because we have not only to hold the bait in the required position but also to deceive the roach into taking it without suspicion. The two aims are not always com-patible, and a great deal of thought is sometimes necessary to arrive at a satisfactory compromise. A golden rule is to use only the minimum of weight necessary to make the tackle work efficiently, and to use the smallest float possible. In some cases, it may be best to dispense with the float altogether and use a leger style of fishing or what is now known as a 'free-line' – a line without float or weight.

This might sound a strange tactic for canal fishing, but it can pay rich dividends. On many occasions I have found myself on the canal bank casting a worm or a large portion of flake into my swim – and even, sometimes, watching the roach take the bait. On other occasions I have used a matchstick for a float or, at dusk, a small white feather. Aided by a following breeze, it is surprising how far this unusual aid to bite detec-tion will travel. The imaginative angler should always be trying to match his tactics to the conditions and to the fish. He should not expect either to conform to some fixed, pre-dictable pattern of behaviour. Fishing is not like that.

While using the feather tactic one bleak winter evening, I picked up twenty-eight fine roach with bread-flake bait – and this after two totally unproductive hours of fishing. No doubt the roach had just moved into the swim; but I would not have been able to discern those bites in the gathering dusk had I been using a normal float. All these roach took the bait while it was sinking – some almost as soon as it touched the water. This activity was in keeping with what I have learned about canal roach, which is that they often become much bolder near dusk, and will sometimes even take baits at surface level.

It is a little more unusual to find roach feeding at surface level during the middle of the day, but sometimes it does happen. On one occasion I can recall, a strong wind was blowing straight downstream, causing considerable drift. About mid-afternoon, I observed several rises on the rolling swell of the waves about twenty yards downstream from where I was sitting. My experiences with river roach indicated that, if these fish were roach, I would have an excellent chance of catching some of them. I started to feed chrysalids into the swim. The rises became more frequent and closer as the fish worked gradually up the trail of baits. They were roach – and I caught twelve of them during the next hour, before they ceased to rise and moved off. The largest weighed one pound five ounces, and the smallest was twelve ounces – fish well worth catching.

The tackle I used to catch these roach off the top was simple but very effective. Two-pound line; a small porcupine quill; and a size 16 hook baited with a floater. No weight was used. The distance between the float and the hook was roughly three feet. I found that if I held back on this tackle and then released it just before the chrysalid reached the feeding area, a roach would rise to it almost every time. (See also Chapter 9.)

This same method can be used with crust as the bait, if the roach are rising. But the sunken bait will usually lure more fish. If it is swum downstream in the familiar style of the river angler, it can be a deadly method for the reed-free straights, especially when used in conjunction with a steady stream of bread-based groundbait.

When the light begins to fade, near dusk, the roach often become much bolder and can often be caught close in, even in the clearest of water, provided that the angler remains quiet and sits well back from the edge of the bank. I can recall many occasions when I have caught roach from virtually under my rod-tip at this time of the day. During the autumn and winter months, the late afternoon is often the best time of all to seek roach in clear water; so much so, in fact, that I rarely bother going out until well after midday. A small piece of crust or flake, lightly fished in the deeper water of the boat-road, will often lure many fine roach at this time of day.

The low temperatures experienced in winter do not necessarily prohibit sport with roach. I have fished through or under the ice below the lock gates and caught many fine nets of roach during the cold months of December and January. Stronger line than that normally used is advisable for ice fishing. The roach might break away by diving under the ice, which will almost certainly cut through weak line. I have used lines of up to six pounds breaking strain in these circumstances, especially when fishing the bait on the bottom, and thus proved what I had long suspected – that fine lines are not always necessary, as I have already intimated, and that one of the reasons why it is often difficult to catch fish from canals is that the angler is sometimes too conspicuous. When there is a layer of ice over the canal and when light penetration is low, as it is at dusk and later, the roach bite more boldly and the matter of line strength is no longer as important as in conditions of clear water and bright sunshine.

Clear water and bright sunshine combine to create what are perhaps the most difficult conditions for successful canal fishing. Without cover, and perhaps even without a meagre growth of reed in the water, the angler is as exposed as if he were alone on a beach in the depths of winter. Under such circumstances, there can be no doubt that very fine tackle and delicate presentation are essential for success with small baits. A line of one pound breaking strain, a tiny quill float and a size 18 hook are often necessary. It is also advisable to compensate for the lack of cover and the increased light penetration by fishing from as far away as possible.

I avoid fishing in such conditions, as far as I possibly can, and concentrate my fishing into the early hours and a few hours before dark. On those occasions when I have fished against the odds, I have found a floating chrysalid or live fly as good a choice of bait as any when the roach are surface feeding. Hemp seed and malt are useful alternatives for below-surface fishing. I believe that, under these circumstances, a bait fished lightly on the bottom, using the lift method, or the flat-float style, is most likely to tempt the better fish. Provided that one sits quietly and well back from the edge of the bank, it is surprising how many roach can sometimes be caught, even in such difficult conditions. The twin

59

enemies are boats and those anglers who spend all their time wandering about looking for someone to talk to.

Straightforward legering is rarely employed by canal anglers, but there are times and circumstances when it is the best method to use. It is particularly effective for across-the-canal fishing in troublesome conditions of wind and strong current, and for fishing the fast water below the lock gates, where the strong current creates the equivalent of a fast-water swim in a river.

There are various ways of assembling a leger rig. I believe the link-leger (Fig 13) is in every way better than the leger weight threaded directly on to the line. The various forms of stop are also illustrated in Figure 13. The split shot is most commonly used; but in my opinion, it is liable to weaken the line seriously.

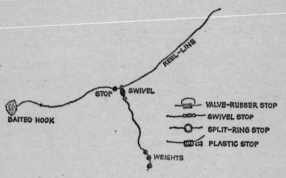

Figure 13. Link-leger tackle with split-shot stop and alternative stops

Rods which are very stiff in action or which have only a flexible tip are not really suitable for this type of fishing. An all-built-cane or fibre-glass rod, ten to eleven feet in length, is ideal. I use my Mark IV Avon and a line of four to five pounds breaking strain. The roach will not usually bother about the strong line in swims of this type if the presentation of the bait is right. The most important point is not to use excessive weight. As long as there is enough on the link to just sink the bait and hold it on the bottom, then everything else should be in order.

I also like to have my rod in a rest and elevated to an angle of roughly forty-five degrees. This creates a 'bow' in the line and keeps most of it above the turbulent surface water. Never have the line taut to the rod-tip. Once the leger has settled in the swim, the line should be reeled in until the lead can be felt and then slightly slackened off again – otherwise the roach will feel the resistance of the rod-tip and reject the bait immediately.

Best baits for this style of fishing are cheese, paste, lobworms and crust. I have caught a great many canal roach while using this method with one of the baits named. The best catch I can remember comprised seventeen roach, all taken on paste fished on a size 8 hook to a four-pound line. The smallest weighed eight ounces, the largest one pound four ounces – good fish by any standards, some of them close to specimen size.

This method of legering can also be used in the 'basins' – those wide parts of the canal where barges were often turned round – and in the canal proper when extremely rough weather makes float fishing difficult. Provided that the bottom is clean, the method I have described will suffice. If there is a thick growth of bottom reed, however, a different arrangement should be used. This is examined in the following chapter.

CHAPTER 6

Roach Fishing the Overgrown Canal

A totally different combination of difficulties faces the angler seeking roach in a heavily reeded canal. The amount of fishable water might consist of only a narrow channel down the boat-road, the shallower parts of the canal extending out from each bank being overgrown with emergent reeds. So intimidating is this mass of reeds that some anglers look once and then turn away, complaining that the canal is not fishable.

Their attitude is understandable but misguided. Such waters can be fished; and they often hold some fine fish, too. Furthermore, although the reeds might complicate the presentation of the bait and make the landing of fish more difficult, there are compensations. The reeds provide cover not only for the fish but also for the angler; and it is often possible to catch roach virtually under the rod-tip, thus eliminating the need for long casting. This must be to the angler's advantage if he adapts his tackle and methods to cope with the conditions.

A long rod is definitely advantageous. I would not normally use one under twelve feet in length when fishing the centre of the canal. A fourteen-foot rod is even better. With a rod of this length, it is possible to reach out and drop the baited hook into the swim with the minimum of trouble – whereas the angler equipped with a short rod might find great difficulty in casting his tackle accurately into the narrow channel beyond the reeds.

Stronger line is also advisable, especially where the fish are of larger than average size. There is little point in hooking fish if you cannot get them out. Two-pound line should be regarded as the minimum. Three-pound is safer. And if the angler has his mind fixed on bigger fish, he should not hesitate to use even stronger line. I often use lines up to six-pound breaking strain when I think the conditions warrant it. Compromise on this issue can be disastrous in terms of fish lost.

The catching of small fish presents no real problem. The same slow-sinking style used in the clear-water canal can be used in the reeded canal, provided that there is sufficient reed-free water to operate it successfully. Using the long rod, it is possible to reach out and virtually lower the tackle into the narrow boat-road. Large numbers of small roach can often be caught like this; and although there is always the possibility that a bigger roach might take the bait, the element of risk can be reduced by fishing the bait only in the upper stratas of water. A pinch of flake or a small maggot should be used as bait.

When larger roach are the quarry, the same style can be used with a slowly falling bait; but stronger tackle should be used, and the baited hook should be set to fall to a greater depth. Remember, hooking the roach might be the easiest part of the operation. Getting the fish out through a dense mass of reeds is the real problem. With this in mind, it is best to find a spot where the reeds grow more sparsely.

I could quote many experiences which would illustrate what can sometimes be achieved with a slowly falling bait, even in these difficult conditions. The one that really stands out in my mind occurred one August afternoon when I took no fewer than one hundred and twenty-five roach in a single afternoon from the Trent and Mersey canal. It was a typical August day: hot and windless. When I arrived at my chosen swim, I was astonished to see an enormous shoal of roach moving upstream between the thick reed-beds. There were, quite literally, hundreds of them – far more than I had ever seen before in one shoal. It was an amazing sight, and I was so astonished that I stood watching them for several minutes before I thought about trying to catch any of them.

By that time, my initial feeling of surprise had lessened and I wondered whether they were feeding roach or whether they were just passing through the swim. I resolved to find out. Keeping well upstream of the shoal, I tossed in several grains of malt and watched closely for a reaction. The result of this preliminary trial was exciting. The advance guards of the shoal snapped up the falling grains avidly, and the interest exhibited by these roach communicated itself rapidly to the remainder of the shoal. They milled and twisted in the clear water, jostling with each other in their eagerness to get to the bait. It was a truly amazing sight to me, remembering those days when it had been difficult to tempt a single fish. I started to fish for them with a grain of malt on a slowly sinking tackle, and by five o'clock I estimated my catch to be in excess of a hundred roach.

Some two hours later, the roach began to move on and bites gradually became less frequent. But I continued to catch fish until near dusk; and this swim – indeed, the whole stretch of this part of the canal for a mile or more downstream – yielded many more excellent catches to me and to other anglers for many weeks after that eventful day.

I do not think, looking back, that this was a day when legering would have rewarded me with as many fish. Nor would a bait fished near the surface, as the roach were not inclined to rise far to the bait. It had to go down to them in as natural a manner as possible, and to achieve this effect I used a small fowl quill weighted with one dust shot, positioned roughly about six inches from the hook. Later on, when the roach began feeding even closer to the bottom, I moved this shot near to the hook; but the basic style remained unaltered.

The same style would not have been suitable for another swim I fished at a later date. This swim was not only lined on both sides with emergent reeds but also had the added complication of clumps of lilies sprouting from the bottom. In between the lilies were small areas of clean gravel, easily discerned because of the clarity of the water. A small shoal of roach was working slowly over the bottom, in between the lilies but not rising above them.

To catch these roach I chose a lightly weighted float-leger rig, so weighted that it would just hold bottom in between the lilies. My bait, as before, was malt. Bites were not frequent, but they came steadily. I caught twenty-five roach from that swim during the afternoon – on a day of dazzlingly bright sunshine. I was well pleased with this achievement. The satisfaction one derives from angling springs not only from the number of fish caught but also from the overcoming of difficulties.

The float-leger style is very useful for holding a bait out in the boat-road if the bottom is clean enough to permit it to be used effectively. The set-up is quite simple. The link-leger described in Chapter 5 is used in conjunction with a float, usually attached by both rings, and set at a depth slightly in excess of the depth of the water. Normally, the tackle is cast out so that the baited hook lies downstream of the float; but in practice I sometimes find it pays to cast the leger *across* the boat-road, so that the baited hook lies close to the reeds which grow out from the opposite bank. The depth at which the float is set must be increased by perhaps as much as two feet, but the method will continue to work efficiently if the float is held on a tight line, close under the rod-tip. I do not mind if it is resting against the reeds in front of me (Fig 14). This method is particularly useful where the current is sluggish.

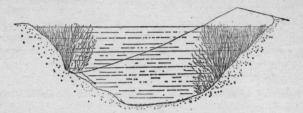

Figure 14. Float-legering across the canal

Another variation is to fish the bait upstream rather than down. The same tackle is used, but the bait is swung upstream. Once the cast has been made, the current may drag the float under. This does not matter. It will surface again, giving a clear indication of a bite when a roach picks up the bait. The method can be improved, in my opinion, by sliding the float up until it is above water. This might sound like a strange reversal of the normal style, but it does work. The pressure of the current now bears only on the line; the bait holds better; and bite indication is just as clear, as the float swings back downstream to a vertical position when a roach picks up the bait. In operation and effect, it is a bite indicator in the swing-tip style. It is important, after casting, to reel in slack line carefully until contact with the leger is just established. The slightest touch from a fish will then dislodge the lead (Fig 15).

The methods I have so far described cannot be used successfully in those areas of the canal where a formidable combination of both emergent reed and bottom reed has to be faced. In many cases, the baited tackle will have to be lowered carefully into the swim and held there on a tight line. The bait must also be kept above the bottom growth of reed, otherwise it will soon become buried and will not be visible to the fish. The slow-sinking style can still be used, but the shotting must be altered to cope with the different conditions. One way of

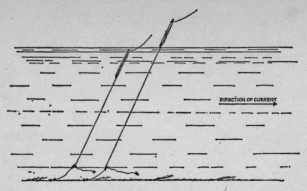

Figure 15. Upstream float-legering with float in and above water

doing this is to bunch the shot at the required depth and then squeeze on one dust shot a few inches from the hook. A trail of at least ten inches is recommended between the bunched shot and the hook. The bait will then sink slowly, but the current will ensure that it does not fall far below the depth fixed by the shot (Fig 16). In this case, the float must be held on a tight line beneath the rod-tip while the bait is sinking slowly down through the water. Some adjustment of weight might be necessary to counter the effect of different currents, but the basic style should remain unaltered.

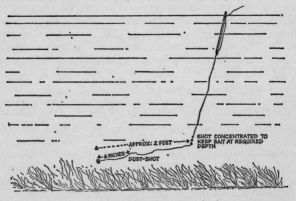

Figure 16. Tackle to keep bait above reeds in strong current

When compared with the slowly falling bait fished in more open water, this method seems more than a little restricted. But in the conditions I have described, the float must be held in a tiny area of clear water and cannot be allowed to move off downstream. If proof of its effectiveness is needed, I can only say that I have caught many fine nets of roach while using it. Bites tend to be sharper; but if the minimum of weight is used to counter the effect of the current, the majority of the bites should be hit successfully.

A different style can be used where the current is very slow or non-existent. It is then only necessary to use a lightly weighted tackle set to fall to the maximum permissible depth – which will, of course, be just above the bottom reed. If crust or flake is used as bait, it is not imperative that the baited hook should remain clear of the bottom. These two baits are buoyant and can be allowed to fall on to the reed, where they will remain visible to any roach in the vicinity. In some cases, where the water is exceptionally clear, the bait can be observed by the angler. All one has to do, then, is to watch and wait for a roach to approach and pick it up. This, again, might sound unusual; but I can assure you that it is sometimes possible to do this. The main requirements are, strangely enough, those

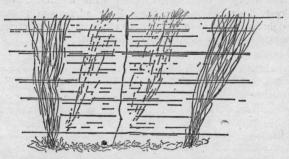

Figure 17. Fishing flake on the bottom in reedy swim

conditions that are often said to be the bane of the canal angler – bright sunshine and clear water. Such conditions permit maximum visibility and are not, in my experience, as destructive of the angler's chances as they are supposed to be. Quietness and concealment are essential, though; otherwise, no fish will be caught (Fig 17),

For across-the-canal fishing with the leger or float-leger,

the rig described in Chapter 5 can be used; but it must be rigged up in a slightly different way. The main difference is that the link must be longer – say, two feet – and the distance between the stop and the baited hook must be shorter. After casting, the slack line should be carefully reeled in until contact with the leger-rig is established. The rod should then be elevated in a rest so that a bow is formed in the line. As soon as this begins to tighten in a positive manner, the strike should be made. (Fig 18).

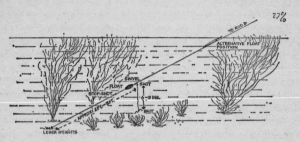

Figure 18. Suggested leger-rig for swim containing both submerged and emergent reeds

To give the rig greater lift, a float can be threaded on – either directly onto the reel-line or onto the link. I use both styles. It is not necessary that the float should be visible. Its object is merely to lift the bait clear of the bottom reed. I think the rig is improved by threading the float onto the link-line rather than on the reel-line, since the line is then left free to run through the swivel without drag. If the float is chosen carefully, so that it just lifts the baited hook clear of the reeds, it will improve the rig rather than detract from its working efficiency. The body of a small antenna float is ideal. It is a good idea to test the rig in the shallows, where it can be seen. The float should rise slowly, bringing the baited hook up with it.

The amount of weight needed on the link-line will vary according to the strength of the current. The one drawback I have encountered is that it becomes difficult to detect bites when there is a strong wind on the water. One solution to this problem is to lay the rod down on the bank with only the tip protruding over the edge. Another, more drastic, method is to thrust the rod-tip under the water and feel for the bites by holding the line between the fingers of the left hand. Great concentration is needed for this, and it is vital that the line should be kept free of intervening reeds. Where there is extensive emergent reed, it is better to fish mainly when the air is calm and still. The method works beautifully then; but it should not be used where normal methods will suffice. It is designed to hold a bait out in a restricted area.

The methods outlined so far seem to take care of most contingencies; but the versatile angler should always remain alert for different ways of overcoming new or existing problems. One method I often use in the densely reeded areas of a canal is to fish a bait on a floatless line. This is a wandering style of fishing rather than a static one. The bait is tossed or lowered into every available area of fishable water, and the line is then hung over the edge of the reed. If the rod is elevated and the line kept clear of the intervening reed, bites are easy to discern. The line slips off the reed and begins to pull taut. Sometimes it may even pull the reed down under the water – an unmistakable indication of a bite. Reasonably strong line is essential for this style of fishing. Three pounds should be regarded as the lowest breaking strain to use. In practice, I sometimes use lines of up to six pounds breaking strain, especially when fishing among lilies. These are a very tough kind of reed. Once roach get among them, they are exceedingly difficult to extricate. The best bait I know for this style of fishing is the worm. If it is used in conjunction with the prebaiting methods previously described, startling results can sometimes be obtained, especially when the water has some colour in it.

All reeds normally encountered in canals are of the rooted variety; but there is one other form of reed-growth which makes only a periodic appearance and has a unique effect on the canal and its fish. This is a floating reed known as duckweed. In shape, its leaves are not unlike those of mustard but with numerous filament-like roots hanging down beneath the surface. In suitably warm conditions, it multiplies at a fantastic rate. It is not at all unusual to see the surface of the canal covered from bank to bank with a solid mass of this reed within a few weeks of it first appearing. This is disconcerting for the angler. It makes fishing difficult, if not seemingly impossible. It clogs up line and float, and hinders both casting and striking. Yet, strange as it may seem, duckweed is also a boon to the angler because it effectively masks off the light from the water. The fish can no longer see the angler on the bank and, as a result, they often bite much more boldly. When I was very young, we used to look forward to the duckweed period because it coincided with some fantastic catches of roach, once we had found a way of effectively fishing through it.

One way is to clear an area of water with an improvised 'boom' which, if left in place, holds back the mass of weed and leaves an area of water comparatively free of reed behind the 'boom'. The fault with this tactic is that it is liable to scare the roach. A better way is to make a small hole in the reed with a stick – a landing-net handle will do – and then quickly lower the baited tackle into the hole. The reed closes around the float quickly, but there is no doubt about the bites when they come: the float disappears. It is a strange, even unique, kind of fishing; but in my experience, it can be very rewarding. I look forward to duckweed fishing.

Nowadays, many canals are overburdened with reed. In others, the reed-cutter periodically brings about an 'improvement' by cutting off the reeds but leaving the roots. Superficially, it appears that a vast improvement has been made; but in reality, the cutter has only solved one problem by creating another.

The exact location of the reed-beds is no longer visible, but the stumps of the roots remain to ensnare any tackle that might be cast among them. The bait must therefore be kept up, off-bottom; and the swimming-down style, with the bait set to remain off-bottom, is the best way I know of dealing with this new situation. There is some compensation in being able to swim the tackle downstream without hindrance and in being able to land any fish caught much more easily. Much of the cover has gone, though; and under these circumstances, the angler is well advised to choose his pitch and to remain there, groundbaiting carefully to attract the roach to him (Fig 19).

During the autumn months, the reeds begin to die off. By the time winter is well advanced, most of them have died. The canal does not then look any different from the clear-water canal, except that it might be more coloured. What is certain is that the bottom will be covered with quantities of decaying reeds. This fact must be kept in mind when bottom fishing, otherwise the bait may be obscured. For this reason, swimming-down tactics, with the bait just clearing the bottom, might be best. But bottom fishing with either chrysalids or bread-baits should also be tried frequently. All of these baits are buoyant and will stay visible above the bottom debris.

When the water is coloured, the roach might often be caught more easily than they are from the clear-water canal. Calm, mild days are best in the winter. If there is a cold north to north-east wind on the water, the chances of catching many roach are limited, in my experience. I would sooner fish through ice than in these conditions.

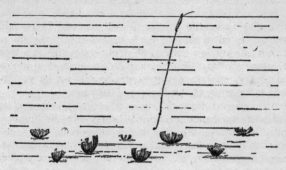

Figure 19. Tackle for fishing after the reeds have been cut

The overgrown canal is really at its best during the summer, though. When the clear-water canal is pierced to its uttermost depths by the brilliant rays of the sun, the reedy canal will often yield plenty of roach to the angler who probes its waters with his chosen bait. Those who turn away limit both their enjoyment and their opportunities. Of that I am quite sure.

CHAPTER 7

How to Catch Big Roach

Some canal anglers are content just to fish. Others fish only for roach. A few set out deliberately to catch specimens. Sometimes their decision is arrived at after a natural progression from small roach to large ones and then, finally, to specimens. Sometimes the change of attitude is brought about by a happy combination of luck and timing which results in the angler catching bigger roach than he ever before thought existed in his canal. He is often surprised – amazed, even. But from that moment on, he is never quite the same again. He will fish with a new awareness, an intenser kind of expectation. He may even, in time, become a dedicated specimen hunter – a man apart; a different breed of canal angler altogether.

Roach of specimen size are not caught easily. Many canal anglers fish their whole lives through and never catch one. It may be that, in some cases, very few specimen-sized roach are to be found in a particular canal. In just a few, there are many such roach. In most canals, they are not common. Any roach over a pound in weight is a good fish; it may even be a specimen for the water in which it was caught. Roach over a pound and a half in weight are very good fish; over two pounds, they are specimens in every sense of the word; and over three pounds, they are truly fabulous fish by any standards.

Finding and catching roach of this class can be a frustrating business. The very uniformity of the average canal – its lack of truly recognizable swims – can be baffling. Where can the angler start to look for them? And more important still, if he succeeds in finding them, how can he single out specimens from the lesser fish and catch them?

The task is certainly difficult, but not impossible. The easiest and most obvious way is to look for them. In canals that are very clear, location by observation is possible; but it takes time, stealth, keen eyes and a lot of patience. The angler who is habitually noisy in his approach and who always precedes his fishing by bombarding the swim with groundbait will seldom catch big roach. An angler who wishes to catch big roach by first spotting them must put traditional canal-fishing tactics aside. The usual match rod, gallons of maggots and fine cloudbait must be replaced by tackle more suited to the needs of the specimen hunter. My own consists of an all-built-cane-rod, twelve feet in length; three-pound line; a tin of hooks; and my baits. Equipped with this tackle, I can travel lightly and quietly up the canal bank, tossing my bait to any fish that I might see.

These tactics do not guarantee big roach, but they do permit the angler to practise a high degree of selectivity. If he can actually see the fish, then much of the uncertainty that normally hampers his efforts is automatically eliminated. Now he can cast his bait accurately to a big roach with the odds against his success drastically reduced.

Prevailing conditions can either hinder or help his efforts. As I have said before, the very conditions which most canal anglers detest – a bright windless day, and clear water – are invaluable allies to the angler trying to spot big roach. In contrast, his chances are lessened when the sky is overcast and the surface of the canal is ruffled by a strong breeze. Locating roach by spotting them becomes impossible then. Another ad-verse factor could be numerous anglers lined along the canal banks. So he must learn to choose his times wisely.

It is best to fish early and late in the day, and preferably with the sun thinly veiled by cloud. Glare on the water makes fish-spotting difficult without polaroid glasses. I learned this quite early in my canal angling days. When seeking good roach, I habitually fished alone – and rarely when there were many other anglers on the banks. At that time, I lived close to a canal and was often on the banks at 5 AM or thereabouts. Legions of roach could often be seen, poised in the clear water like the advance guards of some army. Among them there were sometimes some good fish, but I seldom attempted to catch these; the competition from lesser fish was too immedi-ate. Instead, I sought more isolated shoals: odd groups of bigger roach that could sometimes be seen drifting idly to and fro above the submerged fronds of reeds. A small worm im-paled on a size 12 hook and fished on a weightless line was an excellent bait for these roach. Many times I watched big roach move to intercept the worm. Sometimes they followed it right down into the dimly lit areas close to the bottom; and when

73

they did, the twitching of the line told me when they had taken the bait. Very seldom did I catch many roach while fishing like this, but those I caught were always good ones in excess of a pound in weight. A few were closer to two pounds. One morning I caught three with a worm bait. They weighed one pound eight ounces, one pound nine ounces and one pound six ounces – as beautiful a trio of fine roach as one could wish for from a canal which many thought held only small fish.

Worms are not the only bait that can be used for this style of fishing. Bread-flake and crust can be used too; but they must be well dampened first, and then cast with great care. The big advantage bread has over the other baits is that it remains visible at a greater depth than the others. Sometimes the roach can be seen taking the bait; but if not, the abrupt disappearance of the white flake is indication enough to strike. I have caught a lot of good roach like this.

Another bait which I have used to catch big roach is the slowly sinking chrysalid. It is not as easy to present as the others because it is almost weightless and must be fished on a very small hook. The addition of some weight is therefore necessary. A dust shot or two will suffice. Alternatively, a small self-cocking float can be used. This is a great aid to casting. Because the line runs freely through the bottom ring, the roach does not feel any resistance from the float (Fig 20). The only fault with this method is the tiny splash caused by the float alighting in the water. This might scare the roach, but the risk has to be taken if long casting is called for. When a closer approach is possible, there is no reason why the chrysalid should not be used without the float.

Albert Oldfield, whose knowledge of big canal roach is reflected in the large number of specimens he has to his credit, has caught roach of up to two and three-quarter pounds by using tactics similar to those I have just described. On one occasion, Albert says, he actually watched big roach rising up through the water to take his chrysalid bait. He has also caught specimen roach with such unusual baits as woodlice, centipedes, grasshoppers and freshwater shrimps – which, of course, figure largely on the diet sheet of roach. They also feed upon nymphs of various kinds, small crustacea, and fragments of reed. Baits such as these are best used when the roach can be seen. In the clear waters of the Macclesfield Canal, Albert Oldfield has often used them with great success.

Experiences such as I have just related are illuminating. Methods and baits which seem unusual – but only because they are out of the rut – can lure roach such as most anglers only dream about. Note that not a scrap of groundbait – that supposedly indispensable item of the angler's equipment – was used.

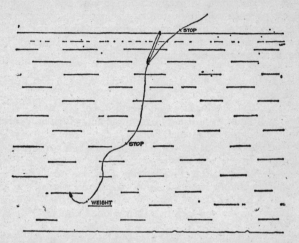

Figure 20. Fishing slow-sinking chrysalid with running self-cocker

This style of angling takes us right back to the beginning: to primitive man, hunting with his spear or bow and arrow, using his eyes to locate his quarry, his stealth to approach it, his accuracy of aim to capture it. The method succeeds because it is simple. It cuts straight to the heart of the problem, without frills or unnecessary complications. There are times when it pays to turn one's back on tradition and habit; to use one's imagination; to try to think more like a fish than a human being. One of the greatest obstacles to success with specimen roach is not lack of equipment, special baits, access to private waters or any of the other reasons which are often advanced, but a refusal to turn away from the habits which cramp and hinder rather than advance the angler's technique and achievements.

It must be admitted, however, that the opportunities to capture roach in this manner can be limited. The water might not be clear enough to permit accurate observation. In some canals, it never is. This complicates matters. Different tactics must be used to capture the unseen specimens. It is also necessary to fish in such a way that the chances of catching immature roach are reduced while the chances of catching the larger ones are advanced.

Rigid rules have little application to any kind of angling; but experience does indicate that the angler who adopts certain procedures will catch more big roach than the angler who fishes haphazardly for anything that might come along. The guides to catching big roach can be summarized thus:

1. Find a secluded spot in which you can fish quietly and alone.
2. Stay alert for any visible evidence of big roach.
3. Refrain from using fine groundbait, which only serves to attract too many small fish.
4. Prebait your chosen swim with the bait you intend to use.
5. Persist in the chosen swim if success does not come quickly (and be sure it will not, on most occasions).
6. Keep well away from favourite hard-fished, reed-free swims unless you can fish them alone at an early or late hour.
7. Find out what times are most favourable to the catching of big roach in your own water.

The last point is of some importance. Roach do not feed for twenty-four hours a day; and although it might be difficult to pinpoint the *exact* time when feeding is likely to commence, experience indicates that early morning is a great time, especially when the swim has been prebaited and the day promises to be hot and bright. During the winter months, when the reeds have died away and the water may be very clear, dusk is the best time. One hour of fishing then might be worth all the other hours together, in terms of bites.

Obviously, then, a lot of time can be wasted by playing the waiting game. The angler who times his visit to coincide with what experience has taught him to be the best time to catch big roach can reduce the time spent at the water side to a mere hour or so. This also means that he will be fishing more alertly, more expectantly. Too much time spent sitting and watching an unmoving float can result in tiredness, both mental and physical, and this is bad. When the chance does come, it may be missed.

A suitable analogy might be found in the case of the game hunter. He could spend many exhausting hours seeking his quarry over a wide area of countryside; but if he knew along which routes his game travelled, and at what times they came down to the water to drink, he could achieve his aim in the minimum of time simply by positioning himself at the water-hole when the game were due.

Unfortunately, anglers cannot always see their quarry or keep track of their movements; so it may sometimes be necessary to lure the roach to an appointed spot by careful and thoughtful prebaiting of the swim. Then the bait can be laid out with some degree of expectation that a good roach may soon find it and accept it. The fast-water swims below lock gates and the stretches of water immediately downstream are often worth trying during the summer. So are heavily reeded swims. Big roach are seldom far away from reeds during hot weather. A cunningly flicked bait might catch one of them unawares, but it is better to prebait the swim if possible. I often do this.

On one occasion, after catching an isolated big roach from a reedy swim, I decided to bait up the swim with whole lob-worms and then fish it early the following morning. I had high hopes of catching some big roach, provided that the swim was left undisturbed until I could return. As it was in a comparatively little-fished stretch of the canal, it was not likely that anyone else would try it.

Next morning, I was back at that swim at 5 AM – having risen early and cycled nearly two miles along the tow-path to get there. It was one of those fine summer mornings when everything was sharply illuminated in that pearly luminosity that sometimes precedes sunrise. My hair and clothes were damp with mist. It was obviously going to be very hot.

I made my first cast from a crouching position, tossing the whole lobworm just over the edge of the reeds and into the boat-road down the centre of the canal. It was taken long before it reached bottom. The line swung away, cutting the water like a knife-edge. I struck and, after a short struggle, hauled out a roach weighing just over a pound.

One hour later, I had eighteen roach. Five of them were over a pound and a half in weight, the largest weighing one pound ten ounces. There was not one really small roach among

77

them; and although none reached the two-pound mark, they were magnificent fish for this canal – far better than those that were normally caught with maggots and tiny scraps of bread. I caught all these fish with a whole lobworm, fished on a size 6 hook to four-pound line. I did not use float or weights, and at least half of these roach took the worm before it reached bottom. When they did not, I merely watched the line for the decisive swinging away that indicated a solid bite.

Several anglers I spoke to afterwards were sceptical. They found it difficult to believe that roach would take a whole lobworm like that. Anglers, in general, seem loath to believe that roach can be taken on anything but the smallest of baits. On the other hand, many specimen hunters closely follow the maxim of a big bait for a big fish. I have no rigid ideas about this myself, but I think that those who insist that one *must* use a small bait are deluding themselves. The big-bait fanatic is closer to the truth. Small roach do not often accept big baits; so some degree of selectivity must be achieved by using a big bait.

I am sure, though, that it is not essential to use a big bait. I have caught many big roach with tiny grains of wheat, malt, or even hempseed and chrysalids, and I have also caught them with big baits: thumbnail-sized pieces of paste, cheese, crust and flake, as well as whole lobworms. The big roach will accept a wide variety of baits of varying sizes. The prejudice against small baits, held by the big-bait angler, seems ill-advised. So is the prejudice against large baits held by the small-bait enthusiast. The secret of success with any bait lies in the avoidance of small roach. With that accomplished, the bigger ones obviously have a greater chance of getting the bait, wherever it is fished.

A relevant question that arises at this stage is whether it is better to fish the bait on the bottom or in a slow-sinking style. In recent years, the idea that one should fish for big roach on the bottom has become so popular that there is now a danger that this, too, will become part of traditional angling lore. It has a basis of truth: the angler who habitually fishes his bait on the bottom will undoubtedly catch some big roach. But it would be wrong to assume that they are always taken there. Looking back over my own experiences, there is no doubt in my mind that big roach can often be caught well off-bottom. I think they tend to feed at whatever level in the water they can find the food organisms upon which they are feeding at the time. This means that they may be found feeding hard upon the bottom; browsing in dense reed-beds; taking nymphs that are ascending to the surface; sometimes even rising to the surface to take food, as they do when taking flies. The angler should seek visible signs of their feeding activities and then adapt his tactics accordingly.

The experiences I have related of taking big roach with a worm or a slowly sinking chrysalid illustrate very well how much can be gained from careful observation and the use of tactics adapted to the needs of the moment. It is also possible for the angler to establish a feeding pattern himself by the manner in which his hook-baits are fed into the swim. If the baits are heavy and sink immediately to the bottom, the roach will obviously tend to feed at that level. If, on the other hand, a slow-sinking bait like flake is used, the roach will begin to move up through the water to accept the flake and may sometimes be caught well off-bottom. Float-fishing tactics should be adjusted to imitate exactly the action of the bait that is thrown in.

In most cases, it is possible to achieve a natural fusion of the two styles. When a lobworm bait is used, for instance, it can be fished on a weightless tackle and it will sink slowly through the water. If it is not taken at this stage, it will sink gradually to the bottom, where it will be vulnerable to any roach feeding there. There is no need to use a lot of weight simply because the bait is being fished on the bottom – unless there is a strong current; and even then, the weight should not be any more than is needed to sink the bait slowly (Fig 21).

A float is optional. I rarely use one for worm fishing. Albert Oldfield likes to use one that is cork-bodied. There may be some advantage in this when the bottom is muddy or reedy. If the depth is adjusted correctly, the float will restrain the worm from burrowing. It is also, of course, a useful indicator. The main objection to its use is that the roach may feel the slight resistance of the float when it picks up the bait. I think it advisable to keep a little slack line between the rod-tip and bait when fishing a floatless and weightless rig. This allows the angler a vital second or so in which to begin striking when the line pulls taut.

I used this method to take five beautiful roach from a clean, gravelly swim one August afternoon. I used bread-paste on a size 8 hook to four-pound line: no float or weights. The bait was simply tossed into the centre channel and allowed to sink gradually between the thick reed-beds. Meanwhile, I fed the swim at intervals with portions of paste, roughly the same size as the paste on my hook. This was one of those occasions when I had to wait for the roach to begin feeding; but feed they did, eventually. After waiting over three hours without a bite, I caught five roach in succession: the smallest weighed one pound four ounces, the largest one pound nine ounces. The following day, I went back to that swim and caught one roach weighing one pound fourteen ounces with what was virtually my first cast.

I have always believed that baits are of secondary import-ance when seeking big roach. Tactics, timing and choice of swim are more important. Nevertheless, certain baits must emerge as clear favourites when a study of catches is made. Most of those I have caught have fallen to lobworms, crust, paste or flake, and only a few to other baits. Lobworms, or lob-tails, are also one of Albert Oldfield's favourite baits. He has caught numerous roach of over two pounds in weight with them, and also a truly fantastic one weighing three

Figure 21. Fishing a lobworm on weightless float tackle

pounds two ounces. This magnificent fish was caught on a lob-tail, fished through a hole in the ice. It is worth noting that Albert had fished that same spot a dozen times before without a bite. Most anglers would have given up. He didn't. This is one of the reasons for his outstanding success.

Albert Oldfield thinks that the lobworm really comes into its own as a bait after a spell of freezing temperatures when, he says, 'the roach are hungry after lying in a state of semi-hibernation'. Personally, I have found crust to be one of the most killing baits during the winter; lobworms are better during the summer and autumn. I think, on balance, crust is probably the most selective bait. Perch love worms, and pike are not averse to them. If you catch a fish with crust during the winter, it is usually a roach. One winter afternoon, while legering a crust bait under the ice below the lock gates, I caught seven roach. The smallest weighed just over a pound, the largest one pound twelve ounces.

The lobworm is most killing when the canal is brimming with coloured water, after a flood or after a thaw, as Albert Oldfield has indicated. I tend to use them more often during the summer because minnows are less troublesome with them than when crust or flake is used. A shoal of minnows can reduce even a large portion of bread to fragments in a few seconds.

Cheese and cheese-paste are fine baits for big roach, too; and I am sure they would lure more specimens than they do if more anglers would use them. Seed-baits will lure big roach if they are persisted with long enough; but in my experience, they are possibly too attractive to the smaller fish. One often catches a lot of roach in the eight-ounce or so category before catching the bigger ones of up to one and a half pounds. Success usually comes after several days of persisting in the same swim; it is not instantaneous, as when using baits like lobworms. If I had to restrict myself to one bait only, I would be hard put to choose between lobworms and crust. Both, in my opinion, are most successful baits in most waters throughout the season. More unusual baits will succeed when, for some reason, the big roach want a change of diet. They cannot always be caught with commonly used baits. The good roach angler does not allow his fishing to fall into a rigid pattern; neither does he become a one-bait man.

Most of the methods and baits I have discussed are well known to most anglers, yet only a minority make full use of them. This partly explains why the majority of roach caught in canals are small; and it also explains why some anglers refuse to believe that big roach can be caught from their local 'cut'. A few are tempted to abandon, for a while, the traditional styles; but when success does not come quickly, they revert to the tried and trusted methods that enable them to catch plenty of small fish. In some cases, they write angry letters to their club secretary or to the angling press deploring the lack of good roach and, sometimes, expressing doubts about the achievements of such anglers as Albert Oldfield. There is often even a demand for restocking. Match results are held up as an indication of the poor quality of the fishing.

Obviously, there must be a reason for such clashes of opinion. Obviously, too, if a dedicated angler can catch big roach from any canal, they must be there for other anglers to catch. The exploits of Albert Oldfield are well known and are beyond dispute. So why is it that one angler can succeed consistently while others seldom, if ever, succeed?

The answer must lie partly in the widely differing attitudes of the specimen hunter and the angler who just wants to catch fish. Albert Oldfield fishes with the confidence of a man who knows that there are big roach to be caught and that he can catch them. His critics are sceptical; their attitude probably influences their efforts to a degree which they would be loath to admit. Also, they do not have Albert's intimate knowledge of the canal and its fish. Possibly, too, almost everything else may be wrong: timing, tactics, baits; and the impatience for results which is the bane of the average canal angler.

The factors that contribute to the success of one angler and the failure of another are not easy to define. The best solution may lie in a stint of searching self-criticism. Somewhere in the unsuccessful angler's attitude or methods there is a defect – perhaps several defects – that he must find and rectify. The gulf between the successful and the unsuccessful may be as wide as a canyon. It can also be hair-thin: a matter of timing, impatience for results, a lack of persistence. These are human faults, and they can be eliminated. Flaws in tackle and presentation can be pinpointed and corrected. But only the individual angler can do anything about his own problems.

CHAPTER 8

Rudd

Most of the styles and baits described for catching roach can also be used to catch rudd. The traditional method is to fish bread-flake in a slow-sinking style, since it is presumed that rudd are more likely to be caught off-bottom than directly on it. In truth, rudd can be caught anywhere between surface and bottom, depending upon where they are feeding at the time. I have caught them with flies, floating crusts, slowly sinking flake or worms, and also with one of these baits lightly legered on the bottom.

Rudd are not common in all canals; in some, they may not exist at all. But wherever they can be found, it is reasonably certain that there will be large numbers of them. I cannot imagine that any canal would contain only a few of them. Like roach, they are shoal fish, moving around in large numbers. I cannot remember ever catching just a single rudd. An odd large specimen might be observed or caught occasionally; but mostly, if you catch one, you will almost certainly catch others.

Small rudd, like small roach, are almost ridiculously easy to catch. Once a shoal moves into the swim and commences to feed, one does not need great skill to build up a substantial catch. A fish a minute would not be a wild exaggeration; in some cases, it might even be an understatement. All that is needed is a plentiful supply of fine cloudbait and a small piece of flake fished in the customary slowly sinking style. The bite rate from a feeding shoal has to be experienced to be believed. Mostly, the fish will be small or medium-sized – of no great interest to the seeker of better fish, but great sport for those who like plenty of action.

Line of around two pounds breaking strain, a small self-cocking float or quill, and a size 14 hook baited with flake could be fairly described as standard rudd tackle for clear-water fishing. Bites are usually easy to detect and should be hit smartly. Rudd can be quick biters, so the float should be shotted well down in the water, leaving about a quarter of an inch of the tip showing. There is no need to use a lot of weight on the hook-length to achieve this effect. Any additional weight needed can be attached just beneath the float or wound around its base in the form of lead-wire. The aim should be to retain the slow-sinking style whatever type of float is used. More weight will obviously have to be used in running water to maintain the slow-sinking effect. I have occasionally taken very large catches of small rudd while using this style in canals where the species is plentiful.

One afternoon in July, I netted sixty-eight rudd with flake. None of these fish was of exceptional size, but I enjoyed catching them. Fishing such as this makes a pleasant change from the blank days one often experiences when seeking specimens.

On this occasion, and on many others I can recall, the rudd were visible near the surface. Sometimes they broke right through, and it was easy to locate them – easier still to choose the logical style to suit the occasion. Not all days are alike, though. There are many days when not a single rudd will be seen anywhere. A deeper-fished bait is obviously called for then. The lift method is an excellent choice of style to catch them from the bottom. So is the loose, sliding float previously described for roach fishing.

Both of these methods are best suited to still-water conditions. Where there is any appreciable current, it is better to bump the bait lightly along the bottom or use a straightforward float-leger style to hold the bait in place. Where the bottom is clean and gravelly, this leger style can be deadly, provided that it is carefully adjusted.

One of my favourite methods of fishing those parts of the canal where there is a brisk current and a clean bottom is to lay the bait lightly on the bottom, using just enough weight to sink the bait and hold it in place. One or two shot squeezed directly on to the line – say, two inches from the hook – can be used. Alternatively – and this is the method I prefer – one small shot should be attached directly to the line, with the others on a separate piece of nylon that is folded over the reel line (Fig 22). The *combined* weight of the stop shot and the other weights should just sink the bait. This is important; and it is a wise tactic to test it in water where the action of the tackle and bait can be seen. Once it has settled on the bottom, a slight lifting of the rod-tip should be sufficient to dislodge the bait and cause it to lift from the bottom. The float should be the smallest possible, and it should be set so that it stays half cocked with its tip just revealed. The bait should lie downstream of the float, directly in line with it. When a rudd picks up the bait, the float will usually lift slightly and then plunge below the surface. It is best to strike as the float lifts,

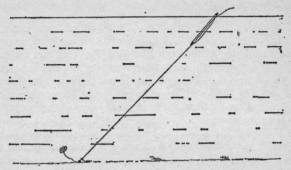

Figure 22. Bottom-fishing method for rudd

although sometimes it may plunge immediately out of sight without any preliminary warning whatsoever. While using this method, I once netted fifty-six rudd, some of which were well over a pound in weight.

Crust and Worm

Floats should not be regarded as being indispensable, though. There is no reason why the baited hook alone should not be used in certain circumstances – as when fishing a floating crust, for instance. This bait can be attached to the hook, cast in and allowed to drift downstream without the aid of a float. Crust and worms can be used together if a two-hook tackle is used. The arrangement is similar to that used when wet-fly fishing. The crust is attached to the tail hook, and the worm to the 'dropper'.

Such a method might seem unusual, but I have found it very useful when fishing shallow gin-clear water in conditions of bright sunlight. The crust acts as a float and is a bait as well. The rudd may take either crust or worm. On one occasion, I caught twenty-five rudd while fishing like this – and on a day when I could see the bottom of the canal quite easily. The largest weighed one pound four ounces.

It is not often necessary to discard a float altogether; but whenever the rudd seem wary of a float-fished bait, this method and the free-line method should be tried. There is no point in sitting fishless when a change of tackle might make all the difference in the world to one's catch.

Weeded Areas

The method just described could not be used successfully in canals where there is a prolific growth of emergent reed. A more restricted method must be used. Provided that the current is not strong, there is no reason why the slowly sinking style illustrated in Figure 6 should not be used. The chances of catching rudd with it are possibly even higher than those when seeking roach, since rudd often lie much higher in the water than roach.

Float-legering styles can be used, too, if the bottom of the canal is not covered with reed and it is necessary to hold the bait in a restricted area. Accessible areas of water between emergent reed might be restricted to a few feet, in some cases, and obviously the bait must not be allowed to drift into this reed.

Where there is extensive reed-growth on the bottom, the baits should be fished so that it will just rest on the reed when it is fully sunk. Crust or flake is the best bait for this style of fishing. Alternatively, whenever the current is strong, the method illustrated in Figure 16 of holding the bait up above the reed should be used.

Live-fly Baits

It is interesting to note that very little attention seems to have been paid to the subject of live-fly fishing for rudd. Since rudd feed extensively off insects, it should be obvious that flies are well worth trying.

The most easily obtained flies are those which can be reared from the maggot stage. They can be roughly classified as blue-bottles, green-flies and common house-flies. Rudd will take all of them avidly. The bluebottle is the largest, and it can be fished on a larger hook than the other two: size 12 is not too big. Green-flies and house-flies, generally smaller, are best mounted on a size 14 or even 16. Sharp fine-wire hooks are essential for successful live-fly fishing.

Maggots turn rapidly into chrysalids and then into flies during the warm summer months. They should be kept in a well-ventilated tin until they are on the point of emerging as fully developed flies. I generally start to use them at that point when the chrysalid can be broken open to reveal the wriggling legs of the fly. At this stage, they can be placed on the hook easily – and the wriggling legs make them even more attractive to the fish. Rudd love them.

When the flies are fully emerged, their wings are not very strong and they can be handled easily enough. Later, as they get stronger, it is best to dampen them by sprinkling water over them. It would be possible to dope them with some kind of insecticide, but I would advise against tainting them in any way. The more natural they look and taste the more likely they are to be taken.

Flies are best fished on the surface on a weightless float tackle which is described fully in Chapter 9 (Figs 23 and 24). The method is most effective when the rudd can be seen rising; but they will often commence rising if the swim is fed with a steady stream of flies. If not, a sunken fly should be tried. I have caught rudd at mid-water levels and off the bottom with flies.

BIGGER RUDD

Singling out the bigger rudd from the smaller ones is not always a simple matter. The baits and methods that catch small rudd will also sometimes catch the big ones. Limited opportunities do occur, if big rudd are spotted and a bait is tossed to them; but this is only possible in the clearest of waters. A pinch of flake or a small worm is the best bait to use for this style of fishing without float or weights.

Live insects or flies will also tempt big rudd during the summer months. But the best all-round bait is undoubtedly flake. Almost all of the larger canal rudd I have caught have fallen to it.

Groundbaiting

In order to catch the rudd, I used the combination of methods and groundbaiting tactics that I have found successful for roach. The fine groundbait is put aside and a heavier form of soaked flake is used. The bait is fished in a style that will allow it to sink gradually to the bottom, and it is then left there. Sometimes it is taken while falling through the water; but more often, it is taken after it has reached the bottom.

Big rudd which fall to this method come usually in one of two ways. Sometimes they follow in the wake of the small fish – which, being more numerous, almost always arrive first – in which case, one often has to endure a spell of catching small fish before the big ones arrive. Or they can be lured into the swim by prebaiting with heavier groundbait; and they can then often be caught much more quickly since the numbers of smaller fish in the swim will be considerably diminished. There is a simple explanation for this. Small rudd are usually much quicker in their pursuit of available food than the large ones; but if they are early to arrive, they also soon depart if there are not enough fine food particles in the swim to keep them interested.

It is often at this stage that the bigger rudd begin to move in. If they are kept in the swim by careful baiting-up with fragments of the hook-bait, it is possible to take a catch in which the large fish will outnumber the small ones. On one occasion, I took fifteen rudd while fishing like this, only one of which was under a pound in weight. The largest weighed two pounds two ounces. Before the bigger fish started to bite, I caught something like thirty small rudd of up to about half a pound in weight. I kept feeding the swim with fragments of flake instead of the customary fine cloudbait, and eventually the tactic paid off.

Another tactic worth trying is to throw quantities of dry bread particles into the swim. Most of this will drift away downstream, sinking very slowly – and it will be followed by the majority of the small rudd, which may often be seen rising to the surface to take the free offerings. This ruse, if successful, considerably diminishes the competition for the bigger particles of bread which are then tossed into the swim with the object of attracting the bigger rudd.

Such ploys do not guarantee results – but they certainly help, especially where there is a perceptible current.

When fishing the still, heavily reeded areas, I would advise against the use of fine groundbait altogether. A large piece of flake fished on a size 6 or 8 hook, together with a careful feeding of the swim with pieces of flake of a similar size, is more likely to bring the desired result. One might have to wait much longer, but the end result could make it worth while. As with all specimen fish, impatience for results is the angler's worst enemy. While pursuing big rudd, I have often returned to the same swim two or even three times to catch the kind of fish I wanted.

Coloured Water

Sometimes, after a period of heavy rain, many canals are coloured by the run-off from the surrounding land; and it is then that a small worm bait is likely to be most successful. If there are large numbers of perch in the water, the effectiveness of the worm bait will be diminished. During a trial period, when I fished with a worm bait exclusively for the greater part of the day, my catch from one canal totalled seventeen perch and only five rudd. When I switched to bread-flake, for the last two hours, there was an immediate change in my fortunes. Every fish I caught from then on was a rudd. In this sense, bread is probably the most selective bait one can use in a canal holding various species.

Problems concerning bait selection are minimal, however, when compared with those of location. In some canals, of course, they are not too formidable. There are canals, notably in Ireland, where an angler can reasonably expect to catch more rudd than any other fish. But it is when a canal holds a mixed population of roach, rudd and other fish that the question of location becomes difficult.

There does not seem to be an easy solution to this. If a shoal can be spotted, the task is simplified. If not, a campaign of exploratory fishing is advisable. By moving from swim to swim, trying each in turn, it is often possible to locate a shoal. Failing that, the law of averages will ensure that a shoal of rudd must be encountered sooner or later by an angler who just fishes the season through with bread-flake as bait. Obviously, though, it is better to find the rudd, and also to seek them in a canal where one has a better-than-even chance of catching them.

RUDD IN IRISH CANALS

For various reasons – one of these being the absence of roach – the canals of Ireland are undoubtedly the best for the seeker of rudd. Unfortunately, many of them are now closed to boat traffic and are overgrown with reeds. The Newry Canal in

County Armagh is still used, to a certain extent, and it holds heavy stocks of rudd. So does the Royal Canal, which flows from Dublin, across the limestone plains to Mullingar; and the Grand Canal, which runs westwards from Dublin and eventually into the Shannon.

Both of the last-mentioned canals are highly alkaline, crystal-clear and heavily reeded during the summer months. Stronger tackle than that normally used is advisable to extract rudd from among the reeds. Care in approach is needed, too. When fishing waters of this nature, I have found it best to find the rudd and then to toss a bait to them or to wait for them, sitting well back from the edge of the bank. Early mornings and evenings, when the light is fading, are the periods when rudd are likely to bite most confidently.

Des Brennan, of the Inland Fisheries Trust, assures me that some reed clearance has been carried out but that the greater part of these two canals is still overgrown. Another point worth noting is that, as there are no locks, the rudd are free to wander over a large area of water, and they often move about a great deal. For this reason, the angler who wanders with bait and tackle, taking a fish here and there, may often be far more successful than the angler who stays put. An excellent tactic, I have found, is to bait up a selected spot and then go on 'safari', returning later to the baited swim to take rudd with a bait carefully and stealthily tossed into the clear water. It does not always succeed, but this tactic works often enough to make it worth trying.

Fellow-angling writer Trevor Housby, who spent some time fishing for big rudd in the Royal Canal, near Mullingar, had some interesting comments to make when I asked him if he would care to pass on any tips for fishing this water. He wrote:

All the big rudd I caught from the canal were taken within ten miles of Mullingar; the best single catch I made amounted to eighteen fish over two pounds in weight. Big rudd were never to be seen in quantity in the canal during the day, but at night they came out in vast quantities, and my usual procedure was to arrive at the waterside at dusk and to fish on until about 1 AM. After this, the rudd tended to go off the feed, probably because, being very shallow, the water in the canal soon cooled.

When I first fished the canal, I used a 'free-line' baited

with flake; but I found that I missed many bites, because the rudd either ran towards me or sucked the flake off the hook without moving it away from its original position. The only way I could overcome this was to use a float, and to trot the bait along just off the bottom. On those nights when there was a bright clear moon, it was possible to watch the float and to strike when a rudd took the bait. On other nights, I fished with the same type of tackle but held a tight line on the float so that I could feel each bite as it came. The rudd were bold biters and did not seem to be deterred by the pull of the rod-tip. [This is true of most fish at night.] The rod I used for this sort of work was a Davenport and Fordham ten-and-a-half-foot trotting rod: a light, easy-actioned glass rod, ideally suited for canal fishing.

I found that the rudd would often hang around any surface reed; and a clump of lilies, even if it consisted of only three or four leaves, would hold the attention of huge numbers of very big rudd. I used flake to take all my biggest rudd – really large pieces mounted on a size 2 carp hook. Smaller baits led to smaller fish, and I did not want these, so I fished with really big chunks. Groundbait was never used as the rudd were already there, so there was no need to attract them or to hold their interest. Bites were always definite on the float, so the actual strike never needed to be hurried.

I caught quite a few rudd of up to one and a half pounds on another stretch of the canal during daylight, but these were caught with maggots which I was using to catch livebait. All the canal rudd were in splendid condition.

As I had not done any night fishing for rudd myself, I found Trevor Housby's comments very interesting in the sense that the seeker of big canal rudd might well adopt night fishing as the first step towards overcoming the problem of catching them from very clear waters. Unfortunately, night fishing is banned in many areas; but wherever it is allowed, it seems that the rewards in terms of big rudd might make the discomfort well worth while.

CHAPTER 9

Dace

Unsuspected numbers of dace lurk in some canals, but they are seldom sought. Most anglers consider the catching of a dace as a freak incident – something that is not likely to happen often, if ever again. Such a conclusion may be true; not all canals hold large shoals of dace. On the other hand, they may evade capture simply because very few anglers ever make a determined effort to catch them.

I fished my own local stretch of the Trent and Mersey Canal for many years before I caught my first dace from it one August afternoon while fishing for roach with bread. The following winter, I caught another while legering with two maggots. This one weighed a surprising eight ounces, and remains the largest canal dace I have caught to date.

After catching this fish, I wondered whether the dace were just odd fish that had somehow found their way into the canal or whether the water actually held a large quantity of them. The answer eluded me until the following summer, when I arrived on the canal bank one afternoon and found the surface dimpled with innumerable rises. They seemed too splashy to be roach; too numerous and small to be chub. It seemed quite possible that these rising fish were dace. I resolved to find out.

Fortunately, I had a tin of chrysalids with me; so I sat down quietly some twenty yards upstream of the rises and commenced to feed the swim with a steady stream of chrysalids. There was an immediate response; then another, and another. Within a few minutes, the centre of the canal was smothered with the tiny rings made by rising fish. Now I was almost sure they were dace. I had only to catch some to be certain.

My hopes were realized in a most convincing manner during the next few hours, for I caught no fewer than forty-five dace from this one swim with floating chrysalids. This success was not easily achieved; nor was I able to repeat it at will. In a sense, it could truthfully be said that I was very fortunate at that time to find a shoal of dace rising freely. Long schooling with the shy dace in my beloved Dove had taught me how to catch them.

The tackle I used then was designed to present the chrysalid as daintily and as enticingly as possible. Dace have keen eyesight, are quick risers, and are often finicky enough to drive any angler to the point of desperation – especially on those occasions when they will take every chrysalid in the swim but the one on his hook. When this happens, it is reasonably safe to assume that there is something wrong with the tackle or with the presentation of the bait. In the clear, slow waters of a canal, dace have ample time to inspect bait that appears in their orbit of vision, and they will reject anything that appears suspicious or unnatural. Fine lines, small floats and tiny hooks are therefore necessary on most occasions. I used one-and-a-half-pound line, size 18 hook and a tiny porcupine quill threaded on to the line through the bottom ring only. To complete this surface-fishing rig, I tied one stop above the float and one below it, about two feet from the hook (Fig 23).

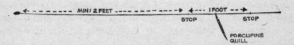

Figure 23. Surface-fishing the chrysalid with small, running float

An alternative method for surface fishing can be arranged by making use of the cork or plastic body of an antenna float (Fig 24). The line is threaded through the body of the float, and the two stops are tied on as before. I think that both this and the loose float method are superior to the bubble float, which is cumbersome, hinders the strike and creates too much water disturbance for successful dace fishing.

As with most other forms of successful fishing, scrupulous attention should be paid to the little things if one wishes to catch canal dace. The first essential is to choose a position from which it is possible to see the swim and yet remain unseen by the dace. Once they have been scared, it may be a long time before they reveal themselves again. The angler who does not stay hidden may ruin his chances immediately. With this in mind, I think it is better to sit on a plastic sheet, low down on the bank, rather than on a stool or basket. Some form of cover which will effectively screen the angler from the fish is also advisable.

The next step is to introduce the bait into the swim as quietly and unobtrusively as possible. A long rod is invaluable for this because it is possible to reach out with it and lower the tackle into the swim. A rod less than ten feet in length is normally quite useless for this style of fishing, especially where there is extensive marginal reed-growth. The long rod eliminates the need for casting, gives the angler close control of his tackle and also lessens the risk of sending a flashing warning signal to the dace downstream.

Once the tackle is in the water, it is only necessary to guide it carefully down the swim, holding it back a little just before it reaches the area where the dace are feeding. This action will ensure that during the vital seconds when the float is travelling into the feeding area it will do so without restriction, because the line will be running through the float, and a dace

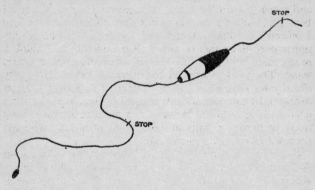

Figure 24. Surface-fishing tackle for dace (float enlarged)

will feel no resistance when it takes the chrysalid. I find it best to watch carefully for the rise and then strike firmly but not violently. Canal dace are not large, but even small fish can break a line if the strike is too fierce.

Another important point is to control the rate at which chrysalids are fed into the swim. The aim must be to get the dace feeding confidently on them, and the best way to achieve this is to keep a thin, steady stream of them going down the swim. If too many are thrown in at once, the dace will follow them downstream beyond effective striking range. In contrast, if the flow of chrysalids is restricted to small, regular quantities, the dace will tend to work gradually up the swim. I have had them feeding virtually under my rod-tip on some occasions.

It is also worth noting that it is better to send the hook-bait down either in advance of or after the feeders – otherwise it will be difficult to discern the hook-bait, or the rise of the dace to it. Of course, the float will give a clear signal of a bite; but if you can actually see the dace rise to the hook-bait, the strike can be made that vital second faster – which means that more fish will be hooked.

Chrysalids are a fine bait for dace, and one of the most selective I know. Even better, sometimes, are the flies that emerge from the chrysalids. Like rudd, dace will often feed upon these madly. The only difference is that the smaller flies should be preferred to the bluebottle. Not because the dace will not take bluebottles. They will. But the smaller house-flies and green-flies can be fished more successfully on the small hook that is often necessary to lure these sharp-eyed little fish. I generally use a size 18, and hook the fly lightly through the upper part of its thorax rather than underneath. I think a much more confident bite results when the hook is above water. The tackle I advised for chrysalid fishing is equally effective for fishing the live fly. The most important thing is to stay quiet and concealed. It is possible, then, to create what is virtually an artificial hatch of flies and get the dace rising freely to them – a truly amazing sight to anyone who has never witnessed such a phenomenon.

Sinkers are naturally better for below-surface fishing than floaters, although the latter can be used if a dust shot or two is attached to the cast. As in roach fishing with a slow-sinking bait, deceptive presentation is very important. The tackle should be as fine as that used for surface fishing. I favour a small porcupine or pigeon quill attached to the line at both ends. These kinds of floats are ideal for canal dace. Heavier tackle and slightly larger floats are only necessary where the current is strong. The depth should be set so that the bait will fall to within a few inches of the bottom; but it is more than likely that it will be taken while it is falling through the water. Provided that there are no obstructions in the form of emergent reed, such tackle can be trotted many yards downstream, and it will help to search out any dace that might be lurking in the swim.

As with surface fishing, dace can be encouraged to feed by sprinkling the swim with sinkers. If there are any dace in the swim, they will soon begin to work up to the source of this supply of food. For this reason alone, it is not wise to move if bites do not come quickly; the angler might well leave the swim when it would have yielded dace had he been patient and remained in his chosen spot. Each kind of fishing makes different demands on the angler. Dace fishing demands not only delicacy of presentation but also alertness and patience, I have, on occasion, caught dace within a few minutes of commencing to fish. On the other hand, I have often had to wait many hours for the first bite.

Slightly different tactics can often be used with excellent chances of success if the swim is completely free of reed – especially if the dace are feeding in the lower stratas of water, close to the bottom. One method is to set the float at such a depth that the bait will trip along the bottom, then cast it out across the canal so that it will drift gradually round in a broad arc until it reaches the shelving slope close in to the tow-path and downstream of the angler. It is well known that dace like a moving bait. This method will sometimes tempt those which ignore a stationary bait or one presented in a slowly sinking style. I can recall at least one occasion when a switch to these tactics brought about a dramatic change in my fortunes. Previously, I had caught only two dace in several hours of hard fishing. Once I had made the change of style, I started to get bites more frequently. By late afternoon, I had accumulated a substantial catch.

It is possible, when something like this happens, that the dace have got their heads down and are grubbing on the bottom for nymphs. The jerky motion imparted to a chrysalid as it progresses across the canal is closely imitative of the swimming motions of some nymphs, and this may be why a dace will take it more eagerly. It is not always possible to observe the dace's feeding habits. There are times when the angler must try to reason things out for himself; to make a decision based upon what he observes and what he deduces. If the dace are not feeding at surface level, they must be feeding below the surface – perhaps, even, right on the bottom. If so, the bait must go down to them; and it must go in an attractive manner. In general, if there is movement in the water, this can be utilized to give life and movement to the bait. If the current is negligible, the angler should make use of whatever breeze there is to impart the necessary movement to the bait. An inshore breeze is a great aid to fishing the chrysalid in the 'tripping along the bottom' style I have just described.

There are times and places where a moving bait cannot be fished, of course. Dace, like roach, are sometimes found in very confined swims. When this is so, any of the styles of fishing previously described for roach in reedy swims can be used. Chrysalids are undoubtedly the most selective bait anywhere; but in my experience, wheat is another very effective bait for dace during the summer and autumn months. Once they have acquired a taste for it, they will often feed on it avidly. This might seem strange; but it should be remembered that fish are imitative in their habits. When one member of a shoal has commenced to pick up the wheat, the others will often follow suit. With careful and prolonged feeding of the swim, a feeding pattern can be established which may last for several hours.

During the winter months, bread-baits and single maggots might be preferred. Both of these baits can be fished in the styles I have described or lightly legered on the bottom, where they will sometimes lure a surprising number of dace – for dace do tend to feed deeper as the season progresses. I have fished for them and caught them at surface level right up until late November, usually during the few hours before darkness when the canal has not been ruffled by a cold wind.

The sunken bait will catch more dace, though – especially during daylight hours; and it is not at all improbable that the roach angler, waiting patiently for the hidden roach to attend his bait, might be surprised to catch a flashing little dace instead. This can happen. It happened to me one October afternoon, and I finished the day with a large haul of dace which I had never originally intended to catch. Next day, that same swim did not yield a single dace. But that is often the way of it with these fish. Small and insignificant they might be, but in other ways, they are a quarry to test the skill and patience of the best of anglers.

CHAPTER 10

Chub

Few anglers associate chub with canals, but they are not as uncommon in these waters as many believe. Several chub of over five pounds in weight have been caught in recent years – including a monster weighing six pounds eight ounces, which was caught from the Basingstoke Canal on legered cheese. Chub of this size could truly be described as exceptional. In canals where chub are common, fish of up to four pounds in weight are sometimes caught.

Locating them can be the major problem. There are no obvious chub swims in canals like there are in rivers; no flood-hollowed banks or undercuts; very few fast runs; and even the overhangs of willows that are almost synonymous with chub are sparse. The other problem is the comparative scarcity of chub in relation to the more numerous roach and perch. This means that, unless some degree of swim selection and bait preference can be established, the capture of chub will remain more a matter of luck than judgement. The problem is even more complicated in canals in which reed growth is scarce or has been cut back. Where, in all this expanse of featureless water, can one begin to look for chub?

The easiest answer is to continue fishing in traditional canal-style and accept any chub caught as a sort of bonus. Chub are caught like this every season, and they are sometimes landed on the finest of tackle. I have caught a few like this myself, including one weighing four pounds two ounces, which I landed on a size 14 hook to one-and-a-half-pound line.

Occasionally, chub are caught in matches; but the majority of canal anglers fish the whole season through without catching a single one. This is not surprising since canal chub are rarely seen, except in the clearest of water. An angler who wishes to catch them must be prepared to dedicate some time and effort to this purpose. I think the first step must be to discard normal canal-fishing methods of angling with maggots for anything that might come along and, instead, begin fishing specifically for chub with the kind of tackle that will ensure that any fish hooked is not likely to get away.

Chub can be landed on fine lines when the swim is free of snags; but even then it is a risky, time-wasting business. They can be landed much more quickly when stronger lines are used. Some really big chub lurk in canals, and I do not hesitate to use lines of up to seven pounds breaking strain when I think it is necessary to do so. Canal chub are not to be caught so easily that anyone can afford to risk losing them through foreseeable tackle deficiences.

Hooks should generally be bigger, too, and preferably eyed. Fine-wire spade-ends are not, in my experience, entirely reliable when a heavy fish is hooked. The objection to using big hooks, often voiced, is difficult to break down, I know; but if there is one canal fish about which this fear of using a big hook is ill-founded it must be the chub. I have caught them on hooks of up to size 1. Provided that a big bait is used to match, the size of the hook is no deterrent whatsoever. The mouth of a chub is large enough to swallow a small orange. Baits the size of a pigeon's egg can be consumed by chub with ease. The only occasion when a small hook is needed is when the bait is also small.

The bait used is of some significance, too. Canal chub do not differ from river chub in their taste for food. The idea that chub will eat almost anything is basically true; but some of the baits that are often listed in angling books – such as cherries, and equally unusual items – can be eliminated for most practical purposes. The outstanding baits for canal chub are the same as those that account for the majority of chub caught in rivers: lobworms, cheese, bread-baits and minnows. Seed-baits can also be very effective if persisted with. But cheese is probably the most selective bait of them all.

I always use cheese in large pieces, and I usually fish it on a size 4 hook. A bait of this size does not necessarily exclude roach and other fish, for a surprising number of roach will accept large pieces of cheese as well as whole lobworms. But the big bait does lessen the chances of catching the very small fish which plague the specimen hunter. Bites will naturally be fewer; and long, blank periods must be accepted as normal. Chub fishing in canals is not like roach fishing. Anglers who are eager for results and think that successful angling is demonstrated solely by the size of their catches should forget chub. This fish is seldom so obliging, or so common.

Rods for chub fishing should be of all-built-cane or fibre-glass and at least ten feet in length. Considerable pressure must sometimes be exerted to bully a big chub out of a reed-bed. This cannot be done satisfactorily with a tip-action rod. For close-range fishing, and for legering, I use my Mark IV Avon in conjunction with lines of from five to eight pounds breaking strain. I also have a longer, twelve-foot, all-built-cane rod to reach out into the more distant swims. A fly-rod is optional but useful.

Floats are an item about which I have no dogmatic views. There are times when I find them indispensable, and other times when I think them an unnecessary encumbrance. They are useful for chub for the same reasons that they are useful for other fish – to hold a bait above the bottom reed, and to drift a bait a long way downstream. The advantages of using a float for this style of fishing should not be minimized. In canals where the water is free of surface reed, a float can be used to cover many yards of water and so, quite probably, present the bait to more chub. Such a tactic, using bread-flake fished on a size 4 hook, brought me three chub one September afternoon. The bait was set to fall within six inches of the bottom, and all of the chub were caught at distances of twenty yards or more downstream.

On this occasion, I had started out to fish for roach. All experienced anglers are familiar with the pattern – one starts out intending to fish for one species, only to end up catching another. Call it luck, opportunism or a happy coincidence of time and place: it does not really matter. The important thing is to take advantage of such heaven-sent opportunities when they arrive. Had I not chosen to fish that particular swim that afternoon, I would probably not have caught chub at all.

The next day, I fished that same swim with identical bait and tactics but failed to catch a single chub. I was not surprised. Catching chub purely by chance is never very satisfactory. It is better, and usually more rewarding, to seek them in swims where one thinks they are most likely to be. One such swim is the fast water below the lock gates. Chub can often be found there, especially during the summer months. The area of water adjacent to the fast water is always worth trying, too, as is the water for some distance downstream.

The fast water is often free of reed; and if the banks are overhung with trees, as they sometimes are, then it is even more likely that chub will be lying along the bank, in or near to the fast, oxygenated water. They can even be seen there sometimes when the water is clear, if the angler approaches the swim quietly and unobserved.

Tactics can be as varied as those used to catch chub in rivers. I have always found it difficult to understand why canal fishing should become a dreary routine of sitting patiently in one spot with a bag of groundbait and a tin of maggots. There is scope for a more enterprising kind of fishing which involves wandering with rod and bait in search of an immediate chance. The fast water below the lock gates and even up in the 'race' itself are ideal places for this style of fishing. A hook baited with a lobworm and then cast up into the fast water, without the hindrance of a float or weight, will sometimes result in the capture of a chub. The method might seem unusual for canal fishing; but these swims are similar to many that can be found in rivers, and there is no logical reason why a method that is so often successful in rivers should not also be successful in canals. The same opportunity for a quick capture is there to be exploited.

The upstream worm cast is one of the best methods I know for catching canal chub quickly. A good alternative bait is cheese. Flake and crust are not good for this style of fishing. Worms and cheese have sufficient weight in themselves to enable a cast to be made upstream with ease. The two breadbaits are lighter and are also apt to fly off the hook. They are both better used when legering, or even for surface fishing. Bread-paste is heavier and is useful in fast water, especially in the winter.

Naturally, the best time to use this method is when the banks are not crowded with other anglers. Early morning in summer is probably best of all. I have often been on the banks at 4 AM, with only a vole for company. Dusk is another time when chub can be caught. Most of the 'bank trampers' will have gone. The light will be fading and chub may be on the move once more, even rising. A floating crust can be a good bait for them when they are near the surface. It can be fished upstream, just like a fly, if the cast is made carefully in an underhand style; or it can be fished downstream merely by lowering it into the fast water and letting the current carry it away. A large piece, at least the size of a penny, should be used. No float or weight is necessary.

This method can also be exploited in the slow-moving parts of the canal; but the chances of catching a chub in this manner decrease as one moves away from the faster water – and one needs a great deal of patience to explore every yard of available water. Nevertheless, the chances do exist. Chub might be lying anywhere in the clear spaces of water. I caught one weighing nearly three pounds one October afternoon when I tossed a lobworm speculatively out into a small hole between a clump of dying reed stems. It was taken at once. The odds against this happening very often are long indeed; but if the method is practised over a long period, a surprising number of chub might be caught.

If the chub can be seen, of course, the chances of catching one are increased. In canals where the water is crystal-clear, the art of spotting and catching visible chub is well worth practising. Stealth and the element of surprise are the angler's allies when using this style of fishing. Groundbait is an unnecessary encumbrance. What is needed, instead, is a keen eye; a rod, line and hooks; landing net; and a tin of baits.

While using this style of fishing, I caught a three-pounder one morning when I surprised it lying just beneath the surface, close to a bed of lilies. I tossed a lobworm to it on a weightless line and caught it within a few seconds. On another occasion, I caught three good chub which were lying beneath a 'mat' of surface reed. I cast the worm across the reed so that it hung down over the edge of it, a few inches beneath the surface, and caught the first chub within a few minutes of making the cast. The others I caught at intervals. Then the bites ceased altogether, and I guessed that any other chub that might have been lying beneath the reed had taken fright.

Patches of reed such as the one referred to often accumulate along the canal during the summer, especially after reed-cutting operations. Chub do not like bright sunlight and will often seek cover when the sun is on the water. For this reason, the reedy parts of the canal are usually best during the daytime.

Observations of this kind are valuable because even if a chub fades away into hiding you know where it has gone, and fishing becomes just that little bit less like a game of chance. If you sit quietly on the bank, the chub will quite possibly emerge again later. Provided that it has not been scared, there is always an excellent chance of catching it either by placing the bait close to its hiding-place or holding back presentation of the bait until it has actually emerged.

The second method is probably the best from the point of view of attractiveness of the bait. If the cast is made lightly and accurately, there must be a good chance that the chub will see it falling slowly through the water and will move to take it at once. I have caught chub with both methods; and I have also watched them nose the bait and turn away from it. It is not possible to succeed all the time. In the last resort, it is the chub that decides whether we succeed or not.

The use of such methods leads inevitably to contemplation of the more static ways of float-fishing and legering, both of which will catch canal chub if used at the proper time and place. Fast water can be float-fished from a position at the head of the swim. But a tiny quill float is of little use for this style of fishing. A large porcupine quill or a goose quill is more suitable. Either of these floats will carry the large shot needed to get the bait down through the turbulent water. The current is often very strong in these swims, and a tiny float carrying only a dust shot or so is swept away downstream quickly, with the result that the bait never gets down to the chub. Lines should be strong, too – of at least three pounds breaking strain.

Legering is preferable when it is desirable to fish the bait on the bottom. The normal style is to fish the bait downstream, using the link-leger method. I would not use line of less than three pounds breaking strain for this kind of fishing, and would not consider six pounds too strong. A big chub hooked in rushing water is no mean adversary and can easily break a fine line. I believe it is a mistake to tie a finer link to the reel line, too. Knots create weak points which are liable to give at the crucial moment; and I doubt very much if the use of a finer hook-link increases one's chances of catching chub. It certainly decreases one's chances of landing them. Use a strong line from reel to hook, and play safe.

Another mistake that is often made is to toss the weighted tackle directly into the swim. This could scare the chub. It is better to toss the bait across the stream and let the current swing it round and downstream. The bait appears much more naturally in the swim, and an immediate take is then possible. A small point, perhaps; but one which can make a great difference to the size of the catch.

Link-legering will only function properly if the weight is adjusted to sink the bait and yet allow it to bump around on the bottom. It should not be so heavy that the bait will sink immediately. A little experimenting might be necessary before the correct amount of weight is found, but it will be time well spent. If the weight is attached to the line by means of a swivel and a separate link, as I have previously described, weight can be added or taken away as required. The same rig can be used in the quieter stretches of water merely by removing some of the weight. In the slow-moving parts of the swim, the weight of the bait alone might suffice.

The upstream variation of legering can also be used in fast swims, but from a different position: not at the head of the swim but from downstream. From there, the bait can be cast upstream and held there. The weight must be just sufficient to hold bottom. When the cast has been made, the rod should be placed in a rest and the line reeled in carefully until all the slack has been taken up. Bites are usually signalled by the line falling slack as the chub picks up the bait and dislodges the weight; but the signal sometimes takes the form of a sharp rap at the rod-tip as the chub darts upstream with the bait.

The float-leger style I advised for roach can also be used, fished either upstream or down, in the quieter water. The upstream method scores because the angler's position, behind the fish, means that he remains unseen. For this reason alone, it is a good method when the sun is on the water. My favourite bait for this style of fishing is cheese, with paste and lobworms as a close second.

Surface fishing with chrysalids and live-flies, previously described, can also be used to catch chub. Mostly, the chub that rise to take these baits are small and can be handled easily enough on fine lines and small hooks; but occasionally, bigger chub do move in and begin to rise to the chrysalids. If this happens, a change to a stronger line must be considered. Line of around three pounds breaking strain is advisable – a reasonably strong line, yet still supple enough to permit deceptive presentation of these small baits.

Most of the chub I have caught with these two baits, and particularly with chrysalids, have been taken on the swim or with the bait laid lightly on the bottom. The latter method, using the emerging fly as bait, can be deadly for chub. I use a larger hook than I normally use for dace or roach. A size 12 is about right. When used in conjunction with a three-pound line and a supple rod, very few chub should escape. I try to avoid heavily reeded swims when using this bait. The finer line and small hook are not really suitable for handling large chub in such conditions.

My method of fishing the sunken chrysalid is quite simple. I attach one shot about two inches from the hook, and then adjust the depth so that the shot lies on the bottom. The float – usually a small quill – is attached by both rings and held on a tight line in the centre of the canal, or wherever the deeper water happens to be. The chrysalid, being buoyant, will remain visible and is more likely to be taken than a maggot fished in a similar style. From time to time, it pays to ease the bait slightly off the bottom by raising the rod-tip. The current then carries the chrysalid a little way downstream. If this tactic is repeated at intervals, a lengthy swim can be gradually searched; and the added movement sometimes spurs a chub into taking the bait. Quite often, other species will take the bait; but this must be expected when using a bait that is attractive to several kinds of fish.

There remains only the question of groundbaiting. I have never believed in the indiscriminate use of groundbait, and in this chapter I have outlined many ways of capturing chub without using it. It can have a useful function, though, if it is of the right kind to attract chub. A groundbait composed of soaked flake or crust, portions of cheese, broken lobworms or one of the seed-baits is best. It should not be dumped into the swim all at once, but introduced gradually and carefully. The aim should be to keep a slow trickle of the bait going down the swim. This will encourage the chub to start picking it up.

Although this tactic does not always have the desired effect, it does often stimulate chub into feeding when they are not actively seeking food. An angler needs patience as well as skill and knowledge. I can recall several occasions when I have caught nothing until the last hour or so; then, suddenly, the chub have started feeding and I have caught one or more within a short space of time.

Even if one's day does not end on this successful note, it is always worth returning to that same swim at dawn the following morning. But do not throw in more groundbait at once. Rather, revert to the tactics described at the beginning of this chapter. Move quietly along the bank, approach the swim from a downstream position and toss in the bait without any preliminary disturbance. A big chub might be lying in wait for just such a tit-bit.

CHAPTER 11

Bream

One summer, long ago, before pollution killed off fine fish, a six-pound bream was caught from the local 'cut'. The average canal bream is much smaller. Fish of up to two pounds in weight are plentiful in most canals, but above this weight they appear to be less numerous. A three-pound bream is a very good fish; a four-pounder could be classed as a specimen; and any bream above this weight is an outstanding fish.

Among the reported captures of exceptional canal bream, the specimen weighing six pounds two ounces caught by Peter O'Dea from the Bridgwater Canal must rank as one of the best in recent years. This fine fish took a float-fished worm. Another fine bream, weighing just over five pounds, was taken from the Oakham Canal, also with a worm, by a thirteen-year-old boy. Such truly exceptional fish are often caught accidently rather than by design. Bream in the four-pound-class are caught more frequently, but not in large numbers. Mostly, they occur as part of a mixed bag of bream which might range from half a pound to two pounds in weight, with only odd larger fish.

In some canals, bream might not exist at all. In others, unsuspected numbers of them could be awaiting the attention of some dedicated enthusiast. Bob Ivey, of the Bream Catchers' Club, says he knows of a stretch of canal not more than twenty-five miles from London which contains bream of a size that would astonish those anglers who think it holds only 'skimmers'. Skimmers, which are very small bream, exist in quantity in many canals and are not difficult to catch once they have been located and encouraged to feed.

Of course, it is easy to say that one is going to fish deliberately for bream; but it is not so easy to put one's ideas into practice. All fish intermingle, to a certain extent; and although bream are shoal fish, it is not at all unusual for an angler who is catching roach with maggots or bread-flake fished 'on the drop' to find that his swim has been invaded by bream. This has happened to me. It has happened to many other anglers. I know of no way that will guarantee that one can always catch bream, and bream only, every time one fishes for them.

Nevertheless, experience has taught me that it is possible, by choosing certain swims and fishing them with methods that are designed to catch bream, to catch them more often than if one merely fishes for anything. The very fact that one has made a deliberate choice of quarry is of some importance because it means that all one's efforts and knowledge of the water are being directed towards the attainment of a specific aim – and this is always helpful. Vagueness and lack of purpose in angling may not be a crime, but they do reduce one's chances of catching specific fish. Observation of bream shoals can also make an important contribution to the total effort. As the angler's knowledge of his chosen water and fish mount, so will his ability to single out and catch his chosen fish increase.

Locating bream in canals is not always an easy matter. The shoals tend to roam up and down the boat-road in search of food. Very rarely will there be only a few bream in any swim. If one bream is seen or caught, it is a practical certainty that there will be others in the vicinity. In the clearest of water, bream can sometimes be seen browsing slowly along the bottom; and sometimes they can be caught by tossing a bait to them or by laying one in their path. I have caught a few like this while using a small red worm on a weightless cast.

I would not advocate this method as a good way of catching a quantity of bream, however. Indeed, when the water is very clear and the sun is bright, bream are often lethargic or shy and can be most difficult to tempt. The dullest days, with low cloud and perhaps a little breeze to ruffle the surface, are better. In general, I prefer not to be able to see my bream. I find they bite more boldly then. They also often bite better at dawn and at dusk. In fact, if the day is bright and there is little wind on the water, my advice to the would-be bream-catcher is to wait until dusk before commencing to fish, or to rise with the lark and get down to the canal before the banks are crowded with other anglers. All my experience indicates that one's chances are much higher at these favourable times.

Groundbaiting in the form of prebaiting can help. I have often introduced groundbait into a swim where I had previously observed bream, and then gone back later to find the bream feeding there. Perhaps I was only able to catch a few of them, but that was not important. The bream had been found and caught. Progress had been made. In my early days, this seemed a great triumph – a big step forward from the time when I merely fished without much hope.

Another lesson I learned was that once the choice of swim was made it paid to persist in that swim for several days if necessary. My experience with canal bream indicates that impatience for results is the bream angler's worst enemy. Probably no other fish, with the exception of the eel, demands such extremes of patience and persistence as this one. Sooner or later, if there *are* bream in the vicinity, they will find the groundbait and start to feed. When they do, there should be no complaints about sport. I have known bream to bite so furiously that the float has scarcely settled in the water before it has sunk away, out of sight.

Methods for bream fishing should be geared to the idea that the bait should usually be fished on the bottom. This does not mean that a heavy weight should be used to plummet the bait to the bottom as quickly as possible; it should only be sufficient to carry the bait through the upper stratas of water, where the very small fish are often shoaling. Bream can sometimes be taken with a slowly falling bait or with a moving one; but my experience indicates that canal bream, whose environment is shallow and often clear, will seldom take baits near the surface. In the clearest of water, during daylight hours, they tend to feed almost exclusively on the bottom – and they should be sought there, unless there are definite indications that they are rising to intercept the bait.

Legering is possible, and it will produce results at the right time. I believe float-fishing methods are generally superior for canal bream, especially where there is little movement in the water. A small carefully adjusted float will register the most delicate bite. Legering is most effective near dusk or after dark, when it becomes difficult to see a float. Bites can be observed by holding the rod up against the sky or by holding the line in the unoccupied hand. This might sound difficult, but it is surprising how long it is possible to go on fishing after the sun has set, if this simple tactic is used. The line can be seen against the afterglow of sunset by a keen pair of eyes.

The terminal tackle for legering for bream should be the same as that for roach and chub: a link, attached to the reel line by a swivel, and weights as needed. The hook should not, in my opinion, be less than a size 12, and it can be as large as a size 6 if a lobworm is used as bait. Line should be of at least three pounds breaking strain – preferably stronger where the bream are known to grow big.

It has been my experience that bream, like most other fish, grow bolder as the light fades. They will then often take baits fished on tackle which they would shy away from during the bright daylight hours. Night fishing would, I believe, produce larger catches of bream – and, quite probably, larger fish too – from those clear waters in which it is often difficult to tempt fish when the sun is on the water.

Along some canals it is said that only the finest tackle and very small hooks must be used to tempt bream during the day. There is a lot of truth in this when the bait is fished on float tackle, particularly if the slow-sinking style is used. In conditions of very clear water and bright sunshine, the choice of line and hook may be crucial. On the other hand, the angler could be under some delusion about this, and will often fish with very fine tackle when there is no case for it. I think it is wise to commence fishing with sensible tackle – say, line of three pounds breaking strain and a size 12 hook – and scale it down only if there are clear indications that the bream are refusing the bait. I have known cases where a change down to something like a one-and-a-half-pound line and a size 16 hook baited with a single maggot has resulted in a definite increase in the bite rate. Conditions vary from day to day; and canals differ from each other, too. The angler must learn to adjust his tactics accordingly.

Float-fishing methods are numerous and varied. Swimming-down tactics often pay off in swims that are devoid of reeds. When used, it is very important to fish the bait at the correct depth. It must not be fished high in the water, so that it passes over the heads of the feeding bream, but should be set so that it just skims the bottom. One shot, at least, should be placed about an inch from the hook (Fig 25). If the float is then retarded slightly while it is progressing downstream, all should be well and the bite will be clearly seen. A large float is not normally necessary. A small porcupine quill, shotted so that only its tip shows, will suffice for this style of fishing. If there is a stiff breeze on the water, it is advisable to sink the line and attach the float by the bottom ring only – otherwise, the float will be blown off course and the bait will behave in a most erratic manner. I have used this method many times to catch bream from canals. It is most effective in clear water, when the bream must often be fished for at a distance. To try to approach them too closely in these conditions can be fatal.

Sometimes, particularly towards dusk, bream do begin to move towards the surface and take a bait as it is dropping through the water. This is especially true of small bream. If the angler wishes to catch them, he must watch carefully for the slightest deviation in the behaviour of the float. If the weights just cock the float or even just sink it when the bait is fully sunk, the slightest deviation in the normal behaviour of the float must be regarded as a possible bite, and the strike must be made. The float may stay flat or move off across the water. These kind of bites are typical of small bream. The larger fish often move off with the bait in a more purposeful manner, which will end with the float sinking out of sight altogether. It is not wise to wait for this to happen, though. The strike should be made at the first positive indication of a bite.

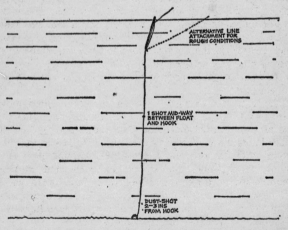

Figure 25. Tackle for swimming-down with bait skimming the bottom when fishing slow-moving water

There are several ways of bottom fishing for bream with a float. If the bottom is clean and the water still, the lift method which I described for roach is perhaps the most sensitive one can use. If the bottom is reedy, the depth at which the float is set should be carefully adjusted so that the bait will just rest on the reed when it is fully sunk. This is very important if maggots or worms are used; otherwise, they will creep into the reed and the bream might not find them. Flake and crust will rest lightly on the reed, so the problem does not arise when they are used.

Tactics for fishing for bream in heavily reeded swims must obviously differ. If the reeds are only of the emergent type and the bottom is clean, a float-legering method using a weight attached to a separate link, which will just hold the bait on the bottom, is as good as any. The amount of weight needed will, of course, vary according to the strength of the current. Some anglers still use a drilled lead for legering, threading the reel line directly through it. This is a traditional method of bottom fishing for bream. I do not like it because of the risk of line fraying through contact with the rough aperture in the lead. Also, I think there is more resistance, owing to the acute angle which is formed between the lead and the rod-tip. The link style of legering allows the bream to pick up the bait several inches before it will feel any significant resistance. There is also far less risk of the line fraying and weakening. Such methods as this are best suited to restricted swims: to the narrow channels between thick beds of emergent reed; and to the clear spaces in beds of lilies and similar types of submerged reed.

Choice of line strength is dependent upon sound judgement based on the prevailing conditions and the anticipated size of the bream. Line of one-and-a-half-pounds breaking strain is normally adequate for catching skimmers and other bream which do not attain great size. For angling in the reedy swims, three-pound line should be considered minimal. Genuine specimen hunters seeking really large bream should not hesitate to use even stronger line. A large bream is no mean adversary in difficult conditions. I have used lines of up to six pounds breaking strain in some swims.

An angler who sets out to catch specimen bream exclusively will have set himself a very difficult task indeed. On the assumption that bream in canals are not greatly different from bream in other waters, it seems to me that the devoted specimen hunter might attain success by closely studying the methods and baits that have resulted in large bream being caught in waters other than canals.

My advice, based on my own experiences, is that it is better, in general, to avoid using methods that are known to catch small bream. Avoid fine groundbaiting. Use worms or paste rather than maggots. Fish these baits on the bottom rather than in a slowly sinking style. Prebait the swim with the bait with which you intend to fish. Choose a time that allows you to fish with the minimum of interruption. And, above all, persist.

In my experience with bream, the smaller fish often have to be caught before the bigger ones move in. In one case, I caught numerous bream of up to two pounds in weight during the first day. During the second and third days, the bigger fish started to come on the feed. Bites were fewer, but I caught several fish of over three pounds in weight, two of over four pounds and one of over five. I could be wrong, but it seems that the normal method of canal fishing – that is, using quantities of fine groundbait and a liberal supply of feeder maggots – is not likely to produce a lot of big bream.

It is often said that heavy groundbaiting is necessary to hold bream in the swim. This may be true to some extent, especially when fishing large still-waters and big rivers. Nevertheless, I think the seeker of really big bream might often find it better to refrain from further groundbaiting with a slowly sinking mixture. The small bream may then begin to move out and the bigger fish, which have been working slowly over the bottom picking up the heavier baits, will begin to move in.

This is mostly theory, I know, but it is theory substantiated to some degree by experience. Looking back over occasions when I have fished the same swim for several days, the bigger fish have often come towards the end of that period. Once, during the third day of fishing in the same swim, I had only two bites on my worm bait all day. I caught two bream weighing three pounds ten ounces and four pounds twelve ounces, respectively. I had not used any groundbait on this particular day, but the swim had been prebaited with a mixture of spent grains, wheatmeal and chopped worms. I have not the slightest doubt that this prebaiting contributed greatly to my small success. I have caught much larger bream from still-waters while using the same tactics – but that is another story.

CHAPTER 12

Tench

Early June mornings, with the mist rising slowly off the water, are traditionally associated with tench. Very few of these fish are caught in the depths of winter, and the capture of a tench weighing three and a quarter pounds by an angler fishing through the ice makes strange reading. Such incidents cause little more than a ripple of surprise in angling circles, though. The pattern of tench fishing in summer, when the temperature is high and reed-growth luxuriant, remains unaltered. Very little of it is done in canals, or in any other water, once the first frosts begin to whiten the banks.

It was once thought that tench hibernated in the mud all through the cold months. Available evidence indicates that this theory is largely false. What is more likely is that tench lie dormant, eating very little and using up a minimum of energy. I once observed a tench lying close to a decaying reed-bed one November afternoon. It did not move when I tossed a stone into the water, and it even allowed me to prod it with my rod-tip. There was no exterior evidence of disease. Eventually, it swam away very slowly. There seemed to be little doubt that this fish was in a semi-torpid state.

In their proper season of summer, canal tench sometimes feed well but are not often seen, except in the clearest of water. They can sometimes be located by signs of 'bubbling' – patches of bubbles rising to the surface, usually in or near reed-beds. If bubbling can be seen, that swim is always worth trying. The bubbles could be caused by bream, but tench are the most likely cause.

I think it would be true to say that tench seldom rise to a surface-fished bait during daylight hours; so for all practical purposes it would be largely a waste of time to look for them at this level. In the clearest of water, they may occasionally be seen cruising through the reeds or, perhaps, feeding off the underside of lilies. But in general, the angler seeking tench should not expect to see them often. They are most likely to be found in or near the thickest of reed-beds, where they can find in abundance the organisms upon which they normally feed. For this reason, the shallow, heavily reeded canals are often best for tench.

Two canals which conform closely to this ideal are the Royal Canal and the Grand Canal, which traverse the great central plain of Eire. They are gin-clear and heavily reeded; and they both hold tench. The late Toby Sinclair, who was an authority on coarse fishing in Eire, advised clearing a swim of reeds prior to fishing. This is often advocated, but I must confess that I have seldom bothered. It is necessary to carry some form of reed-cutting gear to do this, and I have never wanted to burden myself with excess equipment. It is certainly worth considering, though. Such well-known experts on tench fishing as Fred J. Taylor and Frank Guttfield are firm believers in the advantages to be gained from swim clearance.

My own experience has revealed that even in the reediest of canals there are many places where it is possible to insinuate a bait into the holes between the reeds. Strong tackle is essential. The tench is a hard-fighting fish, and it is fool-hardy to risk fine tackle in places where it has only to plunge a few inches into the reeds to escape. Four-pound line should be regarded as minimal, even if the fish are not specimen size.

In those areas of the canal where reed-growth is slight, finer tackle can be used if desired. Tench – even big tench – are sometimes landed by anglers using fine tackle, who are usually fishing for small roach. But such incidents should not be taken as a yardstick by which normal tench-fishing methods can be judged. Any angler who deliberately seeks tench should use tackle which will ensure that he has a good chance of landing any fish hooked. Even in the clearest of water, I would hesitate to use a line of less than two pounds breaking strain.

The fishing of reedy swims breeds a healthy respect for good fish of any species; and since the majority of the tench I have caught from canals have come from reedy places, it is not surprising that I should advocate the use of stronger lines than those normally used by canal anglers. Perhaps, to some extent, I have caught more tench from this type of swim because I have always deliberately sought them there rather than where the absence of reed-growth makes fishing much easier. So it is possible that I might have caught more tench from clear water had I concentrated on that type of swim instead. Nevertheless, I am convinced that the angler who seeks tench in the heavily reeded areas of the canal will catch more than the angler who puts his comfort first.

Reedy swims naturally vary according to the type of reeds that grow in a particular area. Dense patches of fern-like Canadian pond-weed, for instance, provide much-favoured habitats. This reed grows very thickly, but there are often holes in it through which a bait can be fished. Failing that, the bait can often be cast over the outer edge of the reed, where it will be clearly visible to tench lying just under the fringes of the reed-bed.

Wherever the more common reed with the spear-like tip grows, clear patches of water are correspondingly more common; and in many such swims there is a narrow fissure of clear water down the centre of the canal. A long rod is obviously a great advantage when tackling a swim of this type. It should be of built-cane or fibre-glass, and at least twelve feet in length. A rod less than ten feet in length is of little use, except for close-range fishing. Accessible swims may be only a foot or so across, and the tackle cannot be placed in these restricted areas of clear water with a short rod. A rod-rest is of great value. Once the tackle has been successfully placed, the rod can be placed in the rest and the float held steady in position.

It is interesting to note, at this stage, how this same problem of catching tench from reedy swims was dealt with by canal anglers at the turn of the century. In his book *An Angler's Hours*, published in 1905, Sheringham reveals how outsiders – gifted, perhaps, with a little more imagination than the locals – solved the problem that had seemed insurmountable. But first he paints the scene:

Every evening the villagers came forth, each armed with a bean-pole, to which was attached a stout window cord, the bung of a beer cask, and a huge hook on the stoutest gimp. A lobworm was affixed to the hook, and flung with much force and splashing about in some little opening amongst the reeds, where it remains until night draws down her veil.

About once a week the villagers have a bite: a bean-pole is lifted by stalwart arms, and a two-pound tench is summarily brought to the bank. The canal here is one solid mass of reeds. No barge has passed this way for many years, and there is no object in keeping the channel clear in Summer. If the angler wishes to fish he must make a clear space for himself with his bean-pole, in two feet of water, not more than six feet from the bank.

The angler from foreign parts has realized these things, and has endeavoured to strike out a new line for himself. A punt and a long-handled rake were borrowed, and a round pool was cleared some twelve yards from the bank. Then groundbait, in the form of innumerable lobworms, was thrown in. The angler is equipped with a rod of twenty feet, made of East India cane. It is heavier than a roach pole, but also much stronger. A light but strong silk line, and a cast of undrawn gut, with one small bullet to cock the float, and a no: 7 hook, complete the outfit.

Equipped with this tackle, the angler 'from foreign parts' caught far more tench than the locals. This is not surprising. With such a long rod, he could not only reach out over the reeds and place his bait accurately but could also remain out of sight. It is noticeable, too, that his tackle was a little more advanced than was that of the locals. A 'bung out of a beer cask, and a hook attached to the stoutest gimp' is not really the kind of tackle with which to fish for tench. 'A bite once a week' is hardly surprising, under the circumstances.

My own rig for tench fishing in reedy swims seldom varies. One weight, which should be just sufficient to sink the bait gradually to the bottom, is squeezed carefully onto the line a few inches from the hook, and the float is adjusted so that it lies at half cock when the weight is resting on the bottom (Fig 26). When the tench picks up the bait, the float lifts and lies flat, then slides slowly away. If the tench are biting very cagily, the lift method can often be used. Wherever the current is very strong, a float-leger rig should be used. This can be fished either upstream or down, as I have previously explained. A yellow- or red-tipped float will show up well in the reeds and is preferable to one with more sombre colouring.

Sometimes I dispense with a float altogether and use only the baited hook. This is ideal for close-range and long-range fishing among the reeds. Accurate casting is needed to reach the distant swims but it is certainly not beyond the capabilities of an angler with any casting skill at all to toss a worm accurately into a small area of water at a range of from five to ten yards. It is obviously better to overcast slightly, in the event of an error being made; the bait can then be eased back into the hole. Underestimating the distance will mean a fresh cast having to be made. Strong line is a clear necessity: six pounds breaking strain, at least. If the rod is elevated in the rest, a bite can easily be detected from a twitching of the line.

I used this method one July morning to catch seventeen tench of up to two pounds in weight. Some of them took the bait while it was sinking through the water – but as I had prebaited the swim, I was not surprised. A shoal of tench had moved into the swim during the night and were obviously feeding there when I commenced fishing. Normally, the opportunities for making quick captures are limited. It is always worth trying this tactic, though, when fishing swims which are known to be the haunt of tench or which have been prebaited.

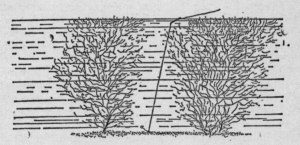

Figure 26. Bottom-fishing rig for tench in reeded swim

I once caught two good tench, one after the other, merely by lowering a lobworm on a weightless cast into a hole in a dense bed of lilies while remaining hidden behind some tall grasses. This succeeded largely because I had baited that little spot with several worms the previous evening, and also because the tench were completely unaware of my presence. In most cases, if the angler commences fishing without any preparation whatsoever, he will have to wait some time for bites to develop. Tench are not noted for their eager biting.

Anglers are not in complete agreement about the value of prebaiting, or about what form it should take. I think it is of great value when seeking tench; and although I do not think it necessary that the groundbait should be composed entirely of the hook-bait, it should certainly have a generous helping of the hook-bait in it. A mixture of greaves and meal was often used in Victorian times. A blend of bread, sugar and maggots is advised by some tench anglers. My own favourite mixture is composed of grains, or wheatmeal, and worms. This sinks quickly and stays where it is thrown.

Differences of opinion also exist about what is the best bait for tench. In my opinion, the best bait is the most selective one. In this sense, the most killing bait for canal tench is the worm. Other fish will take it, but it is more selective than maggots or bread; and if it is fished on the bottom in the kind of swim I have described, the chances of catching tench must be increased. I am undecided only about the relative value of the lobworm and the small red worm. Both will lure tench. The small worm is possibly more effective in very clear water, mainly because it can be fished on a much smaller hook than the lobworm. For the same reason, a single maggot is sometimes successful when the bigger worm remains untouched. The largest catch of canal tench I have ever taken – twenty-five fish ranging in weight from half a pound up to two pounds – was taken on small red worm from a reedy swim which I had fished for three successive days.

The liking of tench for reeds does not mean that they can never be caught in clear water or in similar conditions created by extensive reed-clearance. They can; but location is much more difficult. By way of compensation, the absence of reeds does mean that finer tackle can be used. It is also advisable in such a situation to fish in a far-off style and take advantage of any cover that might be available. The lift method is good where there is little or no movement in the water. A float-leger rig or a straightforward leger is preferable in strongly moving water where there are no complications in the form of thick bottom-reed growth. The style must then be adjusted to hold the bait up over the reeds, as previously explained.

I must confess that I have not done a lot of tench fishing in these conditions. Most of those I have caught from clear-water swims have come along while I have been seeking other fish, mostly roach, using malt or wheat as bait. Tench like these baits, too, and sometimes move in to feed. If this happens, one can do little else but concentrate on fishing for them as long as they stay in the swim. They are not caught so easily that one can afford to shrug off such a heaven-sent opportunity.

The search for specimen tench in canals poses a lot of

problems. It is not likely that they exist in large numbers in the majority of canals. Given favourable circumstances, tench can grow to specimen size, and their growth rate can be rapid. A rate of four and a half pounds in six years has been quoted. It is doubtful, though, if the thickly populated waters of most canals provide the conditions that are essential for such rapid growth. If tench are numerous, it is likely that they will be of small average size – even stunted in growth. If they are not numerous and the conditions are favourable, they may grow much bigger but will be correspondingly difficult to catch. Big canal tench must rank among the most elusive of fish, and it is not likely that the fantastic eight-and-a-half-pound fish caught by Maurice Foode from the Leicester Canal will ever be beaten.

I have never caught a tench of specimen size from a canal, but this is a branch of angling to which I intend to devote more time whenever the opportunity occurs. The main obstacle is locating a water from which one has at least a fair chance of catching a specimen. Canals that hold specimen tench are not common, and many of those taken from canals are caught by accident rather than by design. One of the best canal tench caught in recent years was from the canal at Leven, in Yorkshire. This magnificent fish weighed six pounds fourteen ounces, and it took two maggots fished on a size 14 hook. Several others of over five pounds have been taken from canals in many different parts of the country; but very few canals produce any quantity of large fish. How much this is due to the lack of suitable water, the renowned wariness of large tench and the lack of effort on the part of most canal anglers is a matter for conjecture. It is possible that many large tench break away from the fine tackle that is commonly used in canals and so are never seen. In other cases, the water may be so rich in natural foods that the tench have little incentive to take the baits that are offered to them. What is even more likely is that the numerical superiority of the smaller fish, and their eagerness to compete for baits, ensures that very few large tench ever get hooked at all. How, then, can anyone expect to catch many of these fish?

Most anglers direct their attention to baits in the hope that one or other of these will prove superior. A study of the baits to which big tench fall does not support this theory. Many tench of up to and over eight pounds in weight have been taken from other than canal waters, and the baits which caught them range from lobworms, red worms and maggots to bread-baits and mussels. Only a minority are caught with any other bait. The only common denominator seems to be that most large tench are caught on the bottom and are often an isolated catch rather than part of a large catch of fish.

The simplest and most obvious way of locating large tench is to look for them. In waters that are very clear they can sometimes be seen; and I am sure it would pay an angler who has a suitable water to hand to look first and fish later. A bait cast to a visible fish might be refused; but at least the chances of it being taken would be much greater than if it were merely fished anywhere, more in hope than expectation. This method also allows the angler to single out the big fish from the small ones – which is far more difficult to do when the water is coloured.

In waters of this type – and there are more of them than the very clear type – the tactics I advised for specimen bream are worth considering. I believe the complete cessation of normal fine groundbaiting to be crucial in the capture of large fish. The aim must be to reduce the nuisance of unwanted small fish and increase the chances of big tench finding and picking up the bait. With this in mind, I feel that a big lobworm, a bunch of maggots or a large piece of bread laid on the bottom in a swim known to hold big tench would be far more likely to lure one of them than the usual groundbaiting with fine cloudbait and pints of small maggots. Groundbaiting does occasionally result in a large tench being caught; but when one considers the number of anglers using it, and then lists the numbers of large tench caught in an average season, it is obvious that it is not very successful.

The time chosen to fish is also of some importance, I am sure, whether one is seeking specimens or average-sized fish. Early summer mornings are practically synonymous with tench fishing, and there is little doubt that early morning and the hour before dusk are the best of all – especially in canals that are very clear.

CHAPTER 13

Perch

Perch are probably almost as common as roach in some canals, yet they are seldom sought by the average canal angler. True, they are often caught by anglers fishing a maggot on a small hook; but they can be caught much more consistently by the angler who makes a determined attempt to seek them out and fish for them with methods and baits that are designed to catch them.

The 'spot them and catch them' method that I described for chub fishing can sometimes be used. Normally, perch are not often seen, except in the clearest of water. Yet their habit of hunting in shoals and striking at fry can make them the easiest of fish to locate. The evidence that this action is taking place is often audible as well as visual. The chopping sounds made by the perch are as familiar to many canal anglers as the sight of fry leaping from the water.

Such an occurrence presents the angler with an unparalleled opportunity to catch perch quickly. Since they are obviously hunting for food, the logical thing to do is to use a live-bait. A small fish – such as a minnow, a gudgeon or a small roach – simply lip-hooked and cast into the path of the feeding perch can be a deadly method of luring them. No elaborate float or paternoster rig is needed. This is a time when simplicity pays dividends; when quickness of action rather than patience is called for. A good substitute for the live-bait is a worm or even the bare hook itself, if it is gold or silver coloured. I have used both to catch perch that were striking at fry.

Another effective method is to use a small spinner to lure the perch. Various patterns and sizes can be obtained. My favourite is the small Mepps-type gold spoon, closely followed by the fly-spoon, which is lighter, and the Voblex spinner. Long experience has convinced me that these spinners will catch perch anywhere.

Some anglers use lines of as low as two pounds breaking

strain to spin for perch. I think this is a bad practice. I never use anything of less than four pounds. Where the perch grow big, it would be risky to use anything of lesser strength than this. It is bad fishing to use fine lines and risk leaving a fish with a spinner embedded in its mouth. The strength of the line does not result in less fish being caught, so there is really no case for the fine line at all. In practice, I have sometimes used lines of up to ten pounds breaking strain without ill effects. A careful and quiet approach is far more important, in my experience.

Opportunities with spinner and live-bait are not confined to occasions when perch are hunting. In fact, although it is not uncommon to witness visible evidence of feeding perch, there are many times when no perch will be seen at all. Spinning and live-baiting must then be conducted on a search-and-find basis. The angler becomes once more a seeker and a hunter rather than a static figure confining his actions to one swim.

It is best, I think, to work upstream rather than down, just as one does when spinning in a river. The direction of the cast should also be up and across. I always try to cast my spoon as near to the opposite bank as possible and then reel it in across the canal on a broad arc, using an alternating fast and slow retrieve. Sometimes the perch will snap at the spinner immediately. At other times, they may follow it right into the bank before taking it. Allowance should be made for the deeper water, where the spinner should be worked more slowly. A dead-bait mounted on a spinning flight can also be tried. Somewhat surprisingly, the sprat – which is often used for pike – will attract perch. I have known perch to break surface, with their dorsal fins bristling, in pursuit of a wobbled sprat.

The numbers of perch caught while searching for them is not usually as great as when they can be observed hunting down fry. But if the method is persisted with, carefully and methodically, a surprising number of perch can sometimes be caught. It is not at all an unusual experience to cover several hundred yards of water without moving a single perch and then catch several in quick succession. At other times, it is a case of an odd fish here and there; and sometimes, of course, no perch at all. Some degree of failure must be accepted as inevitable. An angler who persists with this method must catch some perch, though. Total failure over a long period would be most unusual.

Live-baiting for perch is usually a more static kind of fishing; but it need not be. The wandering method employed with a spinner can be used as a means of locating the perch before beginning to fish for them; and there is no reason why a live-bait should not be substituted for the spinner. The mathematical odds against an angler finding a shoal of perch by chance in several miles of water are long indeed. Any tactic that will shorten those odds must be highly desirable. An hour or so spent searching with a live-bait can do just that.

The method employed differs somewhat from spinning. Live-bait will usually dive immediately for the nearest cover. The tackle must therefore be rigged to prevent this from happening and to keep the live-bait visible and vulnerable. Where there is little or no reed at all, I sometimes mount my bait on a floatless line. This is possibly the nearest one can get to natural presentation of a bait, so it is not surprising that it often leads to a high number of immediate runs.

Since a float is not used, the line must be watched carefully for any unusual movement that might indicate a strike. This is usually signalled by a significant speeding up in the line's rate of descent, and sometimes by a sudden cessation of movement. Allow a few seconds for the perch to take the bait into its mouth, then strike. Some perch may be missed – but if the signal given by the line is overlooked, the ratio of missed fish will be even higher. If the slack line is taken up very carefully, the perch can sometimes be felt at the end of the line. On no account should the live-bait be kept on a tight line. If it is the perch will probably eject it at once.

The other method of live-baiting makes use of a float, which should be set at such a depth that the live-bait will be prevented from gaining the shelter of the reeds or the bottom. I think the choice of float is of critical importance. Any old float will not do. The less resistance it offers to the perch the better it will function. Ideally, the live-bait should be able to pull the float down to its tip but not submerge it.

My own choice is a small running float that I make myself from cork and a hollow plastic tube. A stop is tied on to the line at the depth to which the live-bait can be allowed to descend. Another stop is then tied about two feet above the hook; and a weight is squeezed on roughly mid-way between this stop and the hook. Alternatively, another shot can be substituted for the bottom stop if needed. This stop prevents the float from sliding down to the hook, and makes casting

easier. Once the bait alights on the water, it can swim off
freely until the float comes up against the upper stop. The bite
is unmistakable. Since the bait cannot itself pull the float
under, a sudden plunging away of the float must indicate a
bite, and the strike can be made with confidence (Fig 27).

Once one perch has been caught, it pays to try again in the
same spot. Perch are seldom alone, and it is not at all unusual
to catch several from the same swim. A waiting period between each run might have to be endured; but the main object
– that of finding a feeding shoal – has been accomplished, and
one can then fish on with a great deal more confidence.

Long experience of canal fishing for perch will enable an
angler to pinpoint favourite spots and return to them again
and again. The water adjacent to reedy shallows is always
worth exploration because such spots are often the haunt of

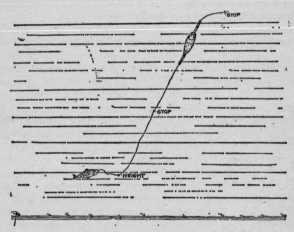

Figure 27. Running-float tackle for live-baiting

teeming thousands of fry, upon which perch feed; and it is
in places such as these that the more static methods of bait
fishing begin to figure importantly in the repertoire of the
seeker of canal perch.

The float-fishing method I have just described can often be
used; but where the swim is confined to a mere hole in a dense
mass of lilies or some other emergent reed-growth, it may be
necessary to anchor the live-bait lightly to the bottom in order

to prevent it from gaining the shelter of the surrounding reeds. A form of paternoster must then be used (Fig 28). This is a well-known method but one which I do not like greatly. However, it is probably the most efficient for these difficult conditions. An alternative is to dispense with the float and use just sufficient weight to hold the live-bait on the bottom, relying solely upon line movement to signal a bite. This works

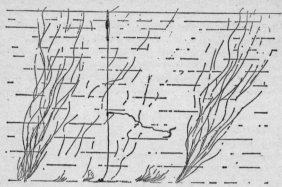

Figure 28. Tackle for perch fishing in reedy swim

well enough where there is no bottom reed, but it is not advisable otherwise. A hidden bait will not attract many perch. Visibility is the vital key to success with perch. They are not essentially bottom feeders, like gudgeon or loach.

At this stage, the use of 'attractors' is worth consideration. I have tried various methods. Chopped fish will attract perch but will also attract eels. Live fish are a better prospect. In this sense, the perch angler may learn something from the deep-sea tuna fisherman who attracts his quarry with cascades of glittering whitebait. A liberal supply of minnows cast into the swim can have a similar if more diminished effect on perch. Many old angling scribes advised imprisoning minnows in goldfish bowls or pickle-jars to attract perch. The idea was that the perch could see the minnows but not touch them. Therefore, it was reasoned, they would be more likely to attack the angler's bait, which was placed near by.

I have not used glass containers. A cheaper container in the form of a polythene bag is now available. If the minnows are imprisoned in this and it is half filled with water, it can be swung out and lowered into the swim impaled on a large hook. Once it has sunk a sharp jerk will free the hook and make a rent in the bag through which the minnows can escape. I think this is preferable to scattering the minnows over the water by hand since it is more likely to concentrate the perch into a small area of water. It is also a most effective tactic in canals where minnows do not exist.

Where minnows are numerous, a liberal use of groundbait and maggots can set up a chain reaction which eventually ends in perch moving into the swim. The groundbait and maggots attract the minnows, and perch are in turn attracted by the minnows. That is the theory – and it is one which, if not infallible, works often enough to make it useful. On the other hand, it sometimes happens that the maggots themselves attract the perch. One might commence catching minnows and small roach and then find, later, that the perch have moved into the swim and are intent on consuming the maggots themselves.

This has happened several times in my own experience. It once resulted in a catch of twenty-three perch, some of which were over the pound mark in weight, all taken on a single maggot with which I had originally intended to catch minnows. Nevertheless, I do not often set out deliberately to catch perch with maggots. Live-baits are probably the most selective bait, with worms a close second choice which I use frequently – both brandlings and lobworms. The brandlings can be fished on a small hook, but the lobworms should be fished on size 6 at least.

Opinions differ as to whether it is better to fish the bait off-bottom or directly on it. In my experience, perch will take a bait at any level. Possibly, the bait fished off-bottom is more effective in most circumstances. The important thing is to make sure that it will not be hidden in any way. Worms tend to burrow; so if the bottom is composed of soft mud or is overgrown with reed, the bait should definitely be fished above the bottom. If, on the other hand, the bottom is composed of gravel or hard clay, the bait can safely be fished on it, either in the float-legering style or merely with one small shot to sink gradually. This last method works well enough where the current is negligible; but where the current is strong, the legering style is preferable.

Off-bottom methods are simple enough, provided that allowance is made for the effect of the current. Where this is minimal, the weight of the bait alone might suffice to take perch anywhere between surface level and a point near bottom. But when the current is strong, the weights should be concentrated to keep the bait up off-bottom in the manner previously described for roach fishing, leaving a longish trail to waver enticingly in the current. The float should be held close under the rod-tip on a tight line. I have caught a lot of canal perch while using this style, baiting with worms.

All of these methods will catch perch. The biggest difficulty is locating them in the first place. The exploratory method with a spinner or live-bait provides one answer to the problem. Another way is to bait up several spots with worms or minnows and then fish each in turn until bites develop. I have found it best to work upstream, laying a trail of baits which will send an enticing scent drifting downstream. If no perch have been encountered by the time the last of the baited spots has been fished, I work back downstream again. It often happens that, by this time, perch have moved into one or other of the baited spots and have begun to feed. When this happens, I keep them interested with odd scraps of worm tossed into the swim, following them with my bait, which is so weighted that it will sink slowly through the water. These methods do not guarantee perch. But they do ensure that one's chances are greater than if one relied upon luck alone. During one period of canal fishing, when I used these methods exclusively, I caught perch four times in six separate visits. This constitutes a very high standard of success indeed. I would have been quite happy to have caught perch on only two of those occasions.

The average size of canal perch is not large. Fish of up to half a pound in weight are quite common. Above that weight and up to two pounds, they are less common but by no means rare. A perch of over two pounds in weight should be considered a specimen, and one of over three pounds would be the fish of a lifetime. Few anglers ever catch perch of this weight from canals. In many cases, it is unlikely that there are sufficient perch of specimen size in the canal to justify any serious attempt being made to catch them. On the other hand, it is also true that there are often more big perch in some canals than most anglers suspect. It needs the determined efforts of an individual, or some unforeseen and unprecedented spell of feeding activity on the part of the perch, to reveal the true extent of their numbers.

One angler who succeeded in topping the magical three-pound mark and even came close to a fantastic four-pound fish was Ken Boulton, who caught a perch weighing three pounds fourteen ounces from the Sandon Canal, near Stafford. It is worth noting that he did not catch it merely by fishing for anything. He had set his mind on catching a specimen perch, and had spent many hours fishing for one before getting the reward he deserved. Not many canal anglers would have risen at 4.30 AM to fish for perch, as he did. Nor would many have chosen to fish with a lobworm on a size 8 hook. Cynics might say he was lucky. Certainly there is always an element of luck in all successful fishing. The methods and baits that will tempt a three-pound perch will also tempt a one-pound perch, or even a half-pounder. Nevertheless, this angler fished in a manner calculated to diminish to negligible proportions the chances of catching small fish, and much of his success could rightly be attributed to that fact.

Another successful angler, whose perch trembled even closer to the four-pound mark, was Trevor Forster, who chipped a hole in the ice covering the Bridgwater Canal to catch a perch weighing three pounds fifteen and three-quarter ounces. This specimen took a minnow; and it was claimed as a record for a canal which, in recent years, has produced an astonishing number of specimen perch. One angler reported the capture of no less than six perch of over three pounds in weight in consecutive casts, and all from the same swim. These, and many others, were taken on a spinner – a method that has lured more perch from this canal than any other.

Results such as these can be misleading in the sense that they seem to indicate that spinning is the best method of catching specimen perch. But it would be reasonable to assume that a method that resulted in the capture of several specimens would soon be adopted by the majority of anglers fishing that water. It is not surprising, therefore, that most of the specimens caught fell to spinners. A broader survey of the baits on which specimen perch have been caught reveals that some have been caught with single maggots, with worms, and with live-baits. My own modest best to date – a two-and-three-quarter-pounder – fell to a live minnow float-fished in a hole in a thick bed of reeds. Spinning offers what is perhaps the quickest way to success, but live-baits and worms certainly should not be overlooked. These baits account for the vast majority of specimen perch caught from canals or any other water.

Wise anglers do not allow the matter of bait choice to obscure the more important matters of time and place. When making a choice of venue, a canal noted for big perch is obviously a better prospect than one which produces few, if any. It is also better to fish in solitude, and at a quiet hour of the day, rather than when the banks are crowded with other anglers. Some good perch are caught infrequently in matches, but they constitute only a minute fraction of the total figure caught throughout any season.

Generally speaking, the summer and autumn months are better for perch fishing than the depths of winter. During the summer, when the reed growth is most luxuriant, I use livebaits and worms for my perch fishing. Spinning really becomes most effective when the reeds begin to die off. The milder months of February and early March can be the best time of all for the seeker of good canal perch.

CHAPTER 14

Pike

There is a widespread belief, which is reflected in the meagre writings on this subject, that canal pike are always small. Possibly, the thought of the cramped environment of a canal gives rise, to a certain extent, to this attitude. Many anglers seem to think that big pike belong exclusively to big waters, but this conclusion is not substantiated by the facts. Very big pike have been caught from smaller waters than canals: from brooks, tiny ponds, ditches and even culverts. There does not seem to be any logical reason why pike should not grow big in canals, too. Food-fish are there in abundance. Hiding-places, in the form of reed-beds, are plentiful. And there are no strong currents to sap their strength. The conditions are, in fact, far more favourable to the growth of big pike than they are in many larger waters; and the reported captures of big pike indicate that they may be more plentiful in some canals than one would suspect.

Several notable pike have been reported in recent years. Pike weighing eighteen and a quarter pounds and nineteen pounds ten ounces have been taken from the Kennet and Avon Canal. One weighing nineteen pounds twelve ounces was caught from the Glastonbury Canal; and a sixteen-pounder was taken from the Taunton–Bridgwater Canal. These are just a few that have been reported. Many others of similar size, and numerous lesser fish, have been caught in many widely separated areas of the country. Indeed, it would be true to say that there are few canals that do not hold some pike – and far more of them would be caught if more anglers fished deliberately for them. Most canal anglers fish only for roach. Very few ever bother to take a pike rod with them.

Smaller pike, in the three- to seven-pound category, are undoubtedly more numerous than the larger ones; and they can provide excellent sport on days when they are feeding well. One October afternoon, while fishing the Trent and Mersey Canal at Alrewas, I was fortunate enough to spot several pike chasing fry in the shallows. This was one of those comparatively rare occasions when the pike could be seen, and it was far too good a chance to miss. I caught three of them with a diving-plug bait. The biggest weighed six and a half pounds. Not large pike by any means: but they provided me with some excellent sport.

Two weeks later, while fishing the same water, I caught a twelve-pound-ten-ounce pike with a Colorado spoon. This fish fought hard and gave me some anxious moments before I finally landed it. To date, it remains the largest canal pike I have ever caught; but I have caught numerous fish of lesser size with baits ranging from lobworms to most of the well-known artificial lures.

Some angling writers advise the use of what is virtually light spinning gear for canal pike: a spinning rod, or a Mark IV Avon; six-pound line; and a small spinner, similar to those used for perch. This sounds reasonable enough, in theory; but I would reject it on the grounds of the possibility of encountering a really large pike. I use a ten-foot built-cane pike rod, and line of ten pounds breaking strain. I think this tackle is preferable because it is normally quite adequate to handle any pike, and the smaller ones are not put off by a slight increase in line strength. Pike are big, strong fish. A powerful strike is needed to set the hooks. The tackle I advocate performs this task much better than the lighter rig.

Methods need not differ greatly from those which are now well known to most pike enthusiasts. Spinners and plugs are both useful – the plug especially since it can be worked on the surface, among the reeds. Pike that take plugs sometimes hook themselves, but a firm strike is advisable to make sure the hooks are driven home.

Plugs should be attached to a wire trace which has a swivel for attachment to the line. They are not as liable to kink the line as spinners, but the swivel will eliminate any risk of this happening. There are many different types of plugs. I like the jointed kind best. They seem ideal where the water is shallow and reedy, because they can be worked on the surface. The diving type are not usually as effective, but they can be useful where there is sufficient depth in the water and when the pike are lying close to the bottom. The best results undoubtedly come when the pike can be seen chasing their prey near to the surface. At such times, they will often grab the plug savagely.

Spinning is another excellent method for both locating and catching pike. An anti-kink vane is essential, however, to prevent line-twist. It should be attached to the line above the swivel. Choice of spinner is a matter of individual preference. There are so many different lures on the market that one could easily spend a lifetime giving each a thorough testing. I do not think pike are too choosy about the shape or colour of the lure. In my opinion, it is the movement of the lure that is so attractive to them. Since they detect their prey through unusual vibrations in the water as well as by sight, they can 'home' on to the source of the vibrations from considerable distances. When they are lying dormant, the spinner might still arouse them; but it will have to be worked closer to them to arouse their latent predatory instincts.

I have caught pike while spinning with fly-spoons and with Devon minnows. Nevertheless, in order to establish some degree of selectivity, I think it best that very small lures should be preserved for perch fishing. There are bigger and better ones for pike.

My preference for large lures is based mainly on the fact that perch will rarely take them. I usually carry a Colorado spoon, which actually spins through the water; a bar-spoon, which weaves and wobbles, giving a fair imitation of a darting fish; and a Voblex spinner, which has eyes and scale markings. I do not think the markings make the last-named more attractive, but it is often a very killing lure in canals. Its only real deficiency is that perch also like it.

Of the innumerable spoons and lures on the market, the ones I have named are my personal choice. Other anglers will have their own preferences. This is of no real importance. What is important is to give each lure a fair trial and not to discard it simply because it does not catch pike the first time out. The next time, that same spinner might tempt several pike.

Spinning tactics should be similar to those used for perch. The spinner is cast out and across the canal and then retrieved erratically, the rate of retrieve being slowed slightly when it is moving through deeper water. Special attention should always be given to the margins, where the reed-beds are usually most dense and where the pike often lie in ambush. When spinning in areas where there is underwater reed-growth, the spinner must not be allowed to sink too far but must be worked over the top of the reeds. A faster than normal retrieve is therefore needed. Even swims where there is a lot of growth in the form of lilies and arrowheads can be tackled; but confident and accurate casting is needed if the spinner is not to become snagged on the tough stalks. Beginners would be well advised to pass such swims by until they are more proficient at casting and retrieving the lure.

The sprat is one of the most effective lures for canal pike; and although the pattern of fishing is very similar to that employed when spinning, it does allow more variation in the style of presentation. As a real fish bait, not a metal lure, it should – in theory, anyway – be more attractive to pike. And experience seems to confirm that it is. Pike of all sizes find sprats very attractive; and the slow-moving water of the average canal is ideal for this kind of fishing.

There are several ways of attaching a sprat. One method is to mount it on a spinning flight, which can be bought from any tackle shop, and then spin it as one would a normal spinner, only more slowly. Another method, and one which will give the bait an entirely different action, is to thread a wire trace – to which is attached a treble hook and a bead or plastic disc – through the vent of the sprat and out at its mouth. The wire trace is then attached to the line in the usual way, by means of a swivel, and the anti-kink lead is added to prevent line-twist (Fig 29). An additional treble or single hook can be placed in

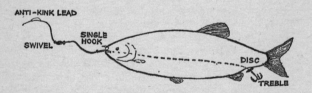

Figure 29. Tackle for fishing with the sprat

the mouth or the head of the sprat, if desired. It will help to prevent the sprat getting torn by the trace, and will also add to the hooking power of the rig. Traces can be bought, or they can be made up from lengths of wire.

A sprat attached in this manner can be retrieved in a series of jerky, erratic movements which are imitative of the actions of a wounded fish. It can also be reeled in more quickly on the surface, working it in and out among the reeds just as one does a plug. This can be a very deadly method indeed for pike that are lying in the reedy shallows. One September morning, I caught seven pike from a heavily reeded stretch of canal while fishing like this.

Yet another method with the sprat is to fish it in a sink-and-draw style – that is, letting it sink, lifting it slowly to the surface and then letting it sink again. This effect is best achieved by threading a weight on the trace and stuffing it into the mouth of the sprat. Alternatively, the weight can be threaded on the line above the trace. The object of the weight is merely to impart a diving motion to the sprat. After casting, the sprat should be sunk and lifted alternately as often as is necessary to work it across the canal. This is most effective when pike are lying deep.

Quite naturally, anglers are usually keen to know which method is most killing. Unfortunately, I do not think it is possible to single out one and say it is better than any other. All of these methods will catch pike. Equally, all might fail to tempt a single fish. No method or bait will guarantee success. The methods can only be made more effective by using each in the circumstances to which it is best suited. The surface retrieve is a natural for shallow, reeded water, and the deeply worked bait, or even one fished in the sink-and-draw style, is best suited to deeper water where reeds are sparse or non-existent.

Those who wish to work a sprat effectively should spend some time watching a wounded or diseased fish, noting carefully how it behaves. When seeking to imitate the activities of living organisms, there is no better way than to study their movements and behaviour patterns. Knowledge gleaned in this manner is of greater value than all the detailed instructions about how to use rod and line. The movements of a wounded fish are easy enough to imitate once they have been observed, and there is literally no movement that cannot be imitated with a sprat.

Live-baiting can also yield good results with pike. Minnows, gudgeon, dace and roach can all be used as baits. A dace or a roach is probably more selective than minnows, which seem to tempt more perch than pike. If pike can be seen, there is no reason why the bait should not be cast to them on a free line – or even lowered into the water close to them, if this is possible. This style of fishing calls for keen powers of observation, a knowledge of the pike's haunts, and stealth on the banks; but the opportunities of exploiting such a method are by no means as limited as one might think. Pike can sometimes be seen striking at their prey, or they might betray their presence by making an unmistakable bulge on the surface. If the bait is then allowed to enter the water quietly, near to the fish, there is every chance that it might take it at once. If not, it is always worth trying a second or third time. Pike are not always inclined to strike at the bait at once.

When using this method, the shallow water close in to the banks should never be overlooked. The fry and other small fish upon which pike often feed congregate in such places, particularly if they are close to reed-beds. Pike know where these fish are, and they often lie in the reeds or close in under the bank, beneath a protective fringe of grasses. Great care in approach is needed to surprise them, though – otherwise, all the angler will see is a monstrous wave hurtling out across the canal as the pike flees for deeper water. Canals are confined waters; and the pike has acute powers of detection. The angler must always remember this and fish with more care than he would when fishing a big, deep lake. The method might sound unusual to those who favour traditional piking approaches, but I can assure anglers that it is worth trying.

When float-fishing with a live-bait, I use a scaled-up version of the rig I advised for live-baiting for perch. The same principles of allowing the bait to swim freely and choosing a float that the bait cannot quite pull under still apply. Pike are not as sensitive to float resistance as other fish, but I do not feel that there is anything to be gained from using an unnecessarily large float. I also lower my bait into the water rather than cast it. This limits the amount of damage done to the live-bait to negligible proportions.

Methods of attaching live-bait are well known to most anglers – although, as one might expect, there is some dissent as to which is the best. For purely humanitarian reasons, I think the large single hook inserted into the lip of the bait is worth consideration. There is definitely a loss of hooking power, though, when compared with that achieved with the more commonly used tackles.

I think the angler should be guided by three considerations when making his choice: to hook the pike firmly; to damage the bait as little as possible; not to hook the pike so deeply that it will suffer irreparable damage. I do not believe in over-burdening any tackle with weights or hooks. There is a happy medium between the single hook and the impressive-looking armoury of hooks that some anglers use. Two sets of trebles should do admirably in most circumstances.

Some anglers place these nearer to the head of the bait than the tail: one set of trebles in the gill slit; the other set in the root of the dorsal fin. Another way is to insert the first set of trebles close to the dorsal fin and in the others close to the tail. The first method can lead to deep hooking. The second is better since the pike swallows the bait head-first and is less likely to be hooked deeply. Timing the strike correctly may be the most important point for consideration. It should not be delayed too long after the pike has made its run with the bait (Fig 30).

Figure 30. Suggested alternative hook positions for live-baiting

Static methods of live-baiting do not produce as many pike from canals as the roving method, in my experience. When roving, the bait is taken in search of pike, and must considerably increase the chances of finding one. With the static method, pike must find the bait – unless, of course, they can be accurately located and the bait placed where they can see it.

However, when a static method is used, I think there are better ways of employing it than leaving the live-bait suspended at mid-water level, swimming round and round beneath a large bung. When the bottom of the canal is clean, as it usually is during the winter months, a much simpler, uncomplicated leger-rig will sometimes lure pike, especially when they are lying deep.

The rig is simple enough to assemble. First thread a swivel on to the reel-line. To the swivel attach, say, six inches of strong nylon, and to this attach sufficient weight to sink the bait. Next, tie on another swivel below the first; this will act as a stop for the link-swivel. To this swivel attach a wire trace, to which is attached a set of treble hooks or one large single hook, as desired. (A ready made-up trace with swivel and hooks attached can be used.) Now it is only necessary to attach the bait and lower it into the swim. When this has been done, the rod should be placed in a rest and the pick-up left open so that the pike can run freely with the bait.

Two sets of trebles can be used, if desired, for greater hooking power. The amount of weight will vary according to the size of the bait used: a nine-inch roach will obviously need more than a gudgeon to sink it. No matter what bait is used, I think it is best to attach only sufficient weight to sink it and restrict its movement. Then, as soon as there is any significant speeding up in the movement of the line, it will be apparent that a pike has taken the bait (Fig 31). A float is not necessary.

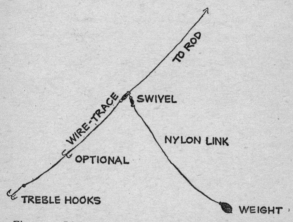

Figure 31. Light legering live-bait tackle for pike fishing

Groundbaiting can help to draw pike into the swim, as most anglers know. In fact, it is not at all unusual for an angler who is intent on fishing for roach to find his swim suddenly invaded by pike. The groundbait attracts roach; roach attract pike. It is a good idea to have a pike rod handy when roach fishing in case a pike does appear. Roach are not likely to stay in the swim long when a pike appears, so the sooner it is caught the better. This is one occasion when I would not hesitate to use a roach live-bait.

Static dead-baits, usually in the form of herrings, have accounted for a lot of large pike in other waters, and there does not seem to be any logical reason why herrings should not produce pike from canals. I must confess that I have not tried this method. The idea of sitting with a dead-bait does not appeal to my somewhat restless nature. I prefer to be active when pike-fishing, seeking them with plug, spinner or wobbled sprat.

The question of inflicting pain does not arise when using dead-bait, of course. For this reason alone, many anglers prefer it. I believe the best way of attaching a dead-bait is to situate the hooks nearer to the tail than the head, if only to lessen the chances of the pike gorging the bait. Two trebles – one placed roughly half way along the bait, the other close to its tail – will do much to prevent this happening, in my opinion.

Anglers who are interested in further exploring the possibilities of dead-baiting might be interested to learn that pike will often take dead-baits fished suspended beneath a float, especially when there is a breeze to move the float across the water and give the bait some semblance of life.

The heads and tails of herring will also take pike. While in Ireland, I was intrigued to learn that some anglers use such baits almost exclusively and have caught many pike with them from still and slow-moving waters. It might at first seem unusual; but on reflection, it is obvious that a bait like this, fished off the bottom, would be less vulnerable to attack by eels. For the same reason, I think it is better to use a whole fish – preferably a large one – when the dead-bait is fished on the bottom.

Canal pike, like pike in any water, do not feed all the time. They are probably influenced more by temperature changes than their brethren in larger, deeper waters. During the winter months, when pike fishing is traditionally in season, the reeds die off rapidly and much of the pike's cover is thus eliminated. The water also often becomes very clear; and during periods of low, freezing temperatures, pike can be very difficult to tempt. The mild, cloudy days are often more productive than the clear, frosty ones, in my experience; and the last month of the season, when the pike are feeding more freely, can be the best time of all.

CHAPTER 15

Eels

Eels could truthfully be called the forgotten fish of canals. Many anglers do not regard them as being true fish at all. Very few ever seek them deliberately. If one is hooked, it is usually more by accident than design; and an eel often has little difficulty in breaking away from the frail tackle used by the majority of canal anglers – which explains why so few are landed. This is a pity. Eels are a worthwhile quarry; and it is likely that there are far more in most canals than is generally realized.

Occasionally, they can be seen. I have sometimes seen them writhing over the shallows; and once, I even hooked one by placing a worm bait in front of it. Such incidents must be regarded as extremely rare, though. Normally, eels remain hidden, their presence unsuspected by all but a few dedicated anglers. A prolonged and carefully planned campaign is needed before significant results can be expected.

The first step to success can be taken by using a bait which eels prefer. Bread-baits, cheese and seed-baits can be ruled out. Maggots will tempt them, but are far too attractive to other species to be really effective. This leaves two baits which lure far more eels than any other: worms, and dead-fish baits. Of the two, dead-baits are probably the best choice of all. Perch and pike will take them. So will chub. But by using this bait, I feel the process of elimination has been taken as far as can be.

Pieces of meat or offal can also be used. Walton advised 'chicken-guts or the guts of any fish', and I have little doubt that these would lure some eeels; but I feel that the dead-fish bait is superior. The Essex specimen hunter Jim Gibbinson – who, with his friends of the National Anguilla Club, has fished extensively for eels in several different waters – shares this view. Jim also believes that dead-baits should be small and fresh.

I agree that the bait should be small. I have found one of the best to be a dead minnow. (I take my baits live to the waterside and kill them there before placing them on the hook.) Eels have small mouths. If a large bait is used, an eel will either pick it up and swim off with it or bite pieces from it, which makes hooking difficult. It is better to use a small bait that the eel can take easily into its mouth. For this reason, bleak, gudgeon, small roach and rudd make excellent dead-baits. My preference for minnow is based almost entirely on the fact that they are numerous in most waters, are easily obtained, and can be regarded as expendable. Large quantities of them can be caught in the minimum of time, and I feel no qualms about using them.

Other anglers might feel that the brightness of a small roach dead-bait would be more attractive to eels. This may be true; but I do not feel that the colour of the bait is significant. All the evidence suggests that eels 'home' on to their food by scent rather than sight. That is why I believe it pays to puncture or cut the dead-bait so that the odour of the fish's juices is released into the water. Wild creatures, including eels, have a far keener sense of smell than human beings and can detect odours in the water at surprising distances. Specimen hunter Bob Church of Northampton discovered this when he baited his chosen pitch with a mixture of raw eggs, pilchard oil and fine soil.

After baiting his swim with this weird mixture, Bob Church caught an eel weighing five and a half pounds, taken on two lobworms – as was another specimen weighing five pounds twelve ounces caught from Whilton Lock, near Northampton. In fact, the majority of the eels taken at this time by Bob Church and his friend Phil Shatford were taken on double lobworms. One could obviously make out a strong case for lobworms on the basis of these captures, but I still feel that a dead fish is the most selective bait one can use. Worms are undoubtedly an excellent eel-bait, but the numbers of other species caught while using them is always much higher than when using a dead-fish bait.

Whether or not the groundbait Bob Church used contributed significantly to the capture of his big eel it is difficult to say. Jim Gibbinson has reservations about the effectiveness of groundbait. It is true that this eel might have been caught had no groundbait been used, but it is my opinion that there is nothing to be lost by groundbaiting – and much might be gained.

A point worth noting here is that Bob Church was fishing a

spot where he had previously been broken by what he thought to be a large eel. I have had this experience too. In my case, I prebaited my swim with handfuls of dead minnows and then returned the following evening to try again with stronger tackle. I caught the eel within an hour – with my hook, which I had lost the previous day, still hanging from its mouth. Inside the eel, I found seven minnows – proof enough that it had been feeding on the minnows I had thrown in. The eel weighed three pounds four ounces.

Minnows and other fish are part of the natural food of eels, so it is not surprising that they should take them. Few anglers would think of crayfish as a bait for eels, though: but Jim Gibbinson and his friends caught eels from the Grand Union that contained crayfish. No eels were caught while using them as bait, however. This seems curious: but it could be that, where crayfish are abundant, other baits might be more attractive simply because they are strange and, in a sense, distinctive. It is of some significance that the canal from which I caught many eels with a dead-minnow bait contained no minnows. This is also true of a gravel-pit from which I have taken many eels with the same bait.

Crayfish can be a nuisance when one is bait-fishing as they will feed on both worms and dead fish. There are times, though, when the bait remains untouched for long periods. Jim Gibbinson has noted that when this is so the capture of an eel is much more likely. Many of the eels caught by members of his group were caught when there was no crayfish activity at all. It could be that crayfish, sensing danger from a feeding eel, scurry rapidly to shelter as soon as their enemy moves into the swim. If so, then a sudden cessation of feeding activity on the part of crayfish could indicate the approach of an eel. Anglers would be wise to stay alert for such an indication.

Locating eels in canals is perhaps even more difficult than locating other fish. Since the eel is so seldom seen, its location and movements must remain largely a matter for conjecture. Canals are ideal habitats for eels, and there are innumerable places where they *might* be found. It is probably best to select a spot and then fish it continuously. I think this is very important. No one can say whether a swim will contain eels at any given time. Nor can one say how long it might take them to find the bait. But find it they will, given time and sufficient inducement.

My method is to prebait a swim with my chosen bait. On the basis that the odds against finding an eel with haphazard methods are long indeed, such a step can shorten the odds enormously. If dead-baits are used, there is also less likelihood of other, unwanted fish being attracted. Selectivity in groundbait is every bit as important as in hook-bait.

Sometimes, in spite of prebaiting and much patient effort, a swim will not produce a single eel. When this happens, it is best to try elsewhere and, by a process of experimentation and elimination, narrow the choice of swim down to a worthwhile few. This takes time and effort; but it must eventually lead to a much higher ratio of success than the kind of fishing which is dependent upon pure chance. A spot which produces one eel will often produce another. Snaggy spots, crevices in the banks and areas of deep, still water are favoured places during daylight hours. Shallow water is generally best avoided, unless it is heavily reeded or close to a hole in the bank where an eel might be hiding.

The time chosen to fish for eels can be important, too. My experiences point emphatically to the warm summer months as being the most productive. Contrary to popular belief, eels can sometimes be caught in the middle hours of the day. I have caught them in the morning and in the afternoon, when the sky has been overcast and the temperature up in the seventies; but from dusk on, after dark, is probably the best time of all. Jim Gibbinson is of the opinion that peak feeding times are one hour after dark and two hours before dawn. One cannot lay down rigid rules about this; but I have found that very clear waters are unlikely to produce many eels during the bright daylight hours. Coloured, reedy waters are a better proposition.

One hot summer afternoon in July, I caught three eels from a prebaited pitch with a legered minnow. They weighed one and a half pounds, two pounds two ounces and two pounds eight ounces respectively. On another occasion, I caught two of over two pounds in weight by legering a minnow close to a barge which had been moored in the basin for several weeks. No doubt, the eels had found a shady haven beneath the barge and were not inclined to move far out during the daylight hours to seek their food.

In *The Compleat Angler*, Walton refers to a method of catching eels which is called 'sniggling'. He makes no particular reference to canals, but his advice to seek eels 'under some covert; or under boards about flood-gates; or weirs or mills; or in holes in the river banks' could be equally applied to canals. 'Take a strong, small hook, tied to a strong line,' he advises, 'and into one of these holes, with the aid of a stick, put in your bait as far as you can. If there be an eel in sight it will bite instantly.'

I have never tried this; but I have caught eels by legering a bait close into the walls below the lock gates. There are many holes and crevices in such places where eels can hide. The setting of dead-lines is prohibited in most areas, of course; and no line may be left in the water unattached to a rod.

The frequency with which bites develop can be indicative of the quality of eels. Big eels are not numerous, and long blank periods between captures must be expected. A large number of 'runs' developing within a short time usually means that the eels will be small. Since very small eels are not really worth catching, the absence of runs should be interpreted as a good sign. On many occasions, I have had only one 'run' in several hours of fishing – but the eel has always been worth catching.

Of course, few anglers would agree as to exactly what is meant by a big eel. Genuine specimen hunters do not get excited about an eel of under three pounds in weight. A four-pounder is judged to be good; and five-pounders are really good. It is eels above that weight that really interest hunters. The average canal angler probably sets his sights much lower. Not all canals hold monsters of the calibre of those caught from the Grand Union. At the same time, any canal might hold eels of unsuspected size. Before members of Jim Gibbinson's group made any attempt to catch eels from the Grand Union, doubts were expressed as to whether the canal was really worth trying. Bob Church thought it was, and caught three eels from it during the first summer. They weighed four pounds twelve ounces, five pounds four ounces and five pounds eight ounces respectively. Rick Gibbinson also caught one weighing five pounds four ounces; and brother Jim hauled out one weighing over four pounds. A truly impressive record of specimen eels for one small group of anglers fishing one canal.

Eels of this calibre could be classed as outstanding; but even if it is suspected that no eels of this size exist in your canal, it is best to fish on the assumption that they might, with tackle strong enough to deal with them. Members of the

National Anguilla Group used lines of up to fifteen pounds breaking strain, and hooks of up to size 2. Few eels could hope to escape when hooked on this tackle, but I feel that it would be extremely risky to use anything of less than five pounds breaking strain line and anything other than a stout, eyed hook.

Rods should be carefully selected, too. The ordinary three-piece roach rod, or match rod, will not do. A ten- to eleven-foot all-built-cane or fibre-glass rod, similar to that used for carp fishing, is most suitable. Long casting is not called for within the narrow confines of a canal, but the eel must be struck hard and hauled out of the swim as quickly as possible.

A Mark IV Avon type of rod will cope well enough when used in conjunction with lines of from five to eight pounds breaking strain; but if lines in the ten- to fifteen-pound range are used, a carp-rod of built-cane or fibre-glass is essential if the outfit is to function efficiently. Match rods, or rods normally used for roach fishing, are definitely not suitable for use with lines of this strength. Attempts with lines in the lower breaking strain range – say, one to three pounds – would only lead to a high proportion of lost eels. This is one issue about which it is impossible to compromise. The tackle must be strong all through.

Weights are not normally required, unless there is an appreciable current. If they are needed, they should be attached to a separate link. The swim bladder of the bait should be punctured; otherwise, the bait might not sink and would be more likely to be picked up by perch or pike.

The method of attaching the dead-bait is well known to most anglers. A wire trace is threaded through the bait, usually in at the vent and out at the mouth. It is then secured to any eyed hook which, in turn, is inserted into the lip of the bait. Another way is to insert the trace through the vent and out near the dorsal fin, where the hook should be lightly inserted. The hook should be eyed, and at least size 6. I favour a size 4. Bob Church and his friends used even larger hooks – up to size 2 or 1/o. Some anglers favour a set of small trebles, which are said to give greater hooking power (Fig 32).

At one period, I experimented with a single hook inserted into the lip of the bait only. Sometimes I retrieved the hook with only the minnow's head on it – but I also caught plenty of eels. It probably succeeded, mainly, because of the smallness of the bait. It would not be as effective when using a large bait because the eel would simply bite pieces from it and would not be easy to hook.

There is a tendency to regard the eel as an insensitive kind of fish that can be caught with the crudest tackle, but I have not always found it to be so. Eels are sensitive both to hooks and line resistance, and they will drop the bait if they find they are unable to move off freely with it. Fortunately, canal-fishing tactics do not require the use of heavy leads, so the tackle can be rigged up to allow the eel to pick up the bait and move off freely. I always leave a long loop of slack line between rod-tip and water, and I keep a close watch on this.

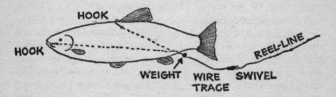

Figure 32. Two hook positions for dead-bait fishing for eels

When it begins to tighten, I usually allow the line to run off the reel freely until the eel stops. Then I wait a few seconds; and then I strike. In extreme cases, when urgent and immediate action is called for – as when the eel is heading directly for snags or a thick reed-bed – I strike immediately. A snagged eel is difficult, if not impossible, to extricate. Some eels are missed through adopting such hasty tactics; but the risk has to be taken – and I usually hook a fair proportion of them when using a minnow.

Once hooked, eels must be bullied out of the swim as quickly as possible. Landing them can sometimes be the most difficult part of the operation. Their length and sliminess make them awkward fish to net in the conventional way with an ordinary-sized landing net. If the bank shelves gradually down into the water, they can be dragged out; but where a net must be used, it should be a large one. Jim Gibbinson and his friends use a forty-eight-inch net which is six feet deep. A net specially designed for eels can be made out of the kind of bag used by greengrocers for onions. The slime of an eel soon makes a mess of ordinary nets. On the same account, a supply of old rag is useful to hold them with. The man who said that eels are more difficult to hold than to catch was not joking.

If fishing is done after dark, the question of bite detection becomes of major importance. On many summer nights, the light never really leaves the sky. If the rod is elevated in a rest so that it is cocked up against the afterglow of sunset, no great difficulty should be experienced in detecting bites. The bites might pull the rod-tip over in an unmistakable fashion; but it is best to watch the line, if possible. The line always gives the first indication of a bite, and it sometimes falls slack as the eel picks up the bait and moves in towards the bank with it. I have known this happen on several occasions; and if I had not remained alert for the sign, I would have missed the bites altogether.

Line movements cannot be discerned when the night is very dark, though, and in this circumstance a bite-indicator is obviously needed. Various forms of electric indicator can be bought, some of which emit a high-pitched buzzing sound when triggered off. Such indicators are very useful if you intend going to sleep. Otherwise, there are several much less expensive methods of bite detection. One of the most popular is to squeeze a piece of silver paper over the line between the reel and the first rod-ring, the line being drawn from the reel and laid loosely on a plastic sheet. If the reel is a fixed-spool type, the pick-up should be in the open position; a centre-pin reel should normally be off the ratchet – but if the rod is pointed directly at the bait, the ratchet can be left on if desired. The device will emit an unmistakable sound when an eel moves off with the bait. When using any of these methods, it is essential to make sure that the line is not caught up anywhere and that its movement will not be impeded by the rest or any other obstruction.

Another method is to hang a large float on the line, using a paper-clip attachment. The float should be coloured with white, yellow or luminous paint so that it can be seen in the dark. If it is hung on the line between any one of the top rings, it gives a clear indication of a bite by lifting as the eel moves off; and the line draws tight.

Normal float-fishing methods are seldom used for eel fishing, but in canals, where one does not have to contend with deep water, there is no logical reason why a float should not be used during daylight hours – or even after dark, if it is of the luminous variety. The depth of water in canals rarely exceeds six feet, and it is usually much less. If the dead-bait is attached as I have described, and the float is adjusted so that the bait lies loosely on the bottom, then a clear, sailing-away type of bite usually develops when the eel moves off with the bait. There may be a few preliminary twitches, but these should be ignored unless a very small fragment of bait is being used. It is my opinion that quicker striking is possible if a small bait is used. I would not use a large fish bait.

Serious eel fishing draws to a close when the first frosts start to whiten the canal banks. It is possible that anyone with the stoic patience to sit out the long cold days might catch eels during the winter, but the low temperatures do not encourage many hours spent motionless on an an exposed bank when there are both pike and perch to be caught. As far as I am concerned, eel fishing will always be connected with the warm days of summer and autumn, when it is a pleasure rather than an imposition to wait on the canal banks for that un-mistakable runs.

CHAPTER 16

Fly-fishing

Fly-fishing in canals must be the least exploited method of all. The appearance of an angler on the banks of a canal with a fly-rod is more likely to provoke derision than any other emotion. It is granted that other methods usually produce more fish; but it is a method that every angler should try sometimes, if only to break out of the rut. Habits, once formed, become hard to break. Rigid adherence to one method can lead to a form of mental stagnation, reducing fishing to a mere routine. The imagination needs to be exercised as well as the casting arm. No harm but much good can come from trying something different.

Dace is probably the species most easily caught with the fly. By nature, dace are surface feeders – darting little fish that often move around in large shoals. I have seen the surface of a canal smothered with the dainty rings made by them. The rise is not usually of long duration. To take full advantage of it, it is essential to be on the canal bank at the right time. There is no doubt in my mind that dawn and dusk are the best times. Dusk is, perhaps, best of all. This does not mean that dace cannot be caught during the morning or afternoon. They can, sometimes. It is not possible to say with certainty when the rise will take place or when it will reach its peak. Experience indicates only that the times I have mentioned are the most productive throughout the season.

Extreme delicacy of presentation is essential in canals. It is difficult enough to deceive this sharp-eyed little fish into accepting an imitation fly in rivers. In the slow-moving and often clear waters of a canal, the problems are intensified. Only the finest of casts and the smallest of flies should be used. The slightest discrepancy or hint of unnaturalness in the appearance of the fly, and it might be refused.

Dry-flies should therefore be tied on small hooks and be well hackled, so that they ride high on the surface. A size 16 hook and a one-and-a-half-pound line would not be too fine.

The fly-rod, too, should be light, and soft in its action. Powerful river or reservoir rods are not needed. A two-piece brook rod, about seven to eight feet in length, is nearer to the ideal. An eight-ounce dace would be considered a real specimen for a canal. The average is probably closer to three ounces. Strong tackle is obviously unnecessary to deal with fish as small as this.

The pattern of fly used is not of critical importance. My favourites are the well-known Pheasant Tail, Blue Dun and Black Gnat. But almost any small fly will be taken by dace. Sometimes they do display a preference, and some experimenting may be necessary before a killing pattern is found. In my experience, such choosiness is rare. The most difficult times to tempt them seem to coincide with the appearance of innumerable black 'smuts', which are impossible to imitate. The dace may feed on these exclusively. If so, no normal pattern of fly is likely to tempt them. Midges will also sometimes produce in them a similar degree of preoccupation; but it is possible to produce a passable imitation of midges with a few white hackles wound sparsely around a small hook. This is probably mistaken for midge larvae rather than actual midges and should therefore be fished hanging just below the surface film.

Wet-flies will tempt dace, too. The rise to a dry-fly can be observed; but with wet-fly patterns, the fly is often invisible, beneath the water, so the cast must be watched closely for any speeding-up in its rate of descent. This might sound difficult, in view of the fineness of the cast, but in practice it is usually easy enough.

If the fly is not taken as it descends, it should be withdrawn slowly to the surface. Dace that take the fly at this stage will probably hook themselves. If this happens, it is not advisable to strike; merely tighten firmly on to the fish, and keep the line taut. A violent strike will almost certainly lead to line breakage.

I cannot emphasize too much how important it is to move quietly along the banks, to cast carefully and lightly, and to withdraw any hooked fish as quickly as possible. Remember that dace are shoal fish. In the absence of a brisk current, it is possible that they may not be facing upstream as they would normally do in a river. Therefore, they will be much more easily scared. Once this happens, the shoal may be lost. A great deal depends upon the amount of fly life that is on the water. If it is prolific, the dace may soon reappear after being allowed a brief rest. The water should never be flogged. More fish can be caught by letting the dace regain confidence after one of them has been hooked.

Roach are somewhat easier to catch, but they do not rise as often as dace. The pattern of the rise is different, too. Whereas the dace is quick and sometimes splashy, the roach rises in a more leisurely fashion and sips in the fly, scarcely breaking surface but rather just dimpling it. This sometimes makes it difficult to see the rise. Nevertheless, roach can often be seen rising, thus giving the angler time to prepare for the strike.

The same patterns of fly used to tempt dace will tempt roach. Wickham's Fancy, Greenwell's Glory and any of the Olives are excellent roach flies, too. As with dace, the pattern of the fly is not as important as the presentation. Dry-flies are most effective towards dusk; but roach often seem to prefer wet-flies or nymphs. These should be fished either in a slow sink-and-draw style, hanging just beneath the surface film, or in a jerky motion suggestive of a swimming nymph. The first style is self-explanatory. The fly is cast out, allowed to sink, then withdrawn slowly to the surface. Roach sometimes take the fly as it is sinking, but they are more likely to take it as it is being withdrawn. I have even known them to follow the fly right into the shallows before taking it. Two flies or nymphs can be used, but I prefer to use only one. This should be dampened before casting to ensure that it will sink. The plastic nymphs which can be bought at any tackle shop will, of course, sink under their own weight. They can be quite effective sometimes, and I have caught a lot of canal roach with them.

Fishing flies or nymphs hanging just beneath the surface film is a method that is not widely used; but in my experience, it can be one of the deadliest of methods for roach when they are rising to take food from the surface. For maximum effectiveness, it is best used when there is a breeze on the water to sweep the flies round in a slow arc. This movement is often very attractive to the roach. As I have said, two flies or nymphs can be used: one on the tail and one as a dropper, about two feet farther up (Fig 33). The cast should be lightly greased, but the flies should be dampened to ensure that they sink. The point of getting them to hang just beneath the surface film is that this is where the roach expect to find live nymphs that are ascending to the surface. I have caught two roach at once while using this method, but that is unusual. The most I ever caught in one session was twenty-eight; the largest of these weighed one pound four ounces and took a March Brown nymph.

Roach are not seen at surface level as frequently as dace, except during the warmest months of the year. They can sometimes be observed somewhere around mid-water level; and if the fly or nymph is allowed to sink slowly down to them, one of them may intercept it. If this does not happen, it is time to try the jerky retrieve which I mentioned earlier. The motion is quite easy. Cast the nymph out across the canal and allow it to sink; then, holding the rod low and in line with the bank, work the nymph gradually inshore with a repetitive jerky motion of the rod, at the same time gathering line in with the left hand. This sounds complicated, but it is simple to put into practice.

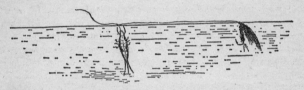

Figure 33. Surface fishing with artificial nymph and wet-fly

The cast is not as important as the way in which the nymph is worked while it is under the water, where it does its work. Fine casting might catch the eye, but it is the nymph or fly that catches the fish. Keep the cast light. Cover each area of water thoroughly before moving on, extending each cast to gradually reach the far bank. The worst mistakes are to thrash the water with numerous unnecessary casts and to hurry on in an effort to cover as much water as possible. It is better to be thorough, and to do everything slowly and methodically. I have caught many roach with this method when there has not been a rise visible anywhere (Fig 34).

Chub are, of course, the largest of canal fish that can be caught with flies, but they are also the most difficult. They are not regular risers; they seldom congregate in large shoals, as dace and roach do; and they are far more wary. Also, they are much stronger. This means that stronger tackle than that used for dace and roach is needed to subdue them. Unfortunately, the use of such tackle may lead to the chub rising to the fly, only to turn away again at the last moment. I have had this galling experience on several occasions.

The simplest solution seems to be to scale the line down to a point where the presentation of the fly is so natural that the chub will take it without suspicion; but such an action can lead to line breakage and the loss of the fish. The risk can be taken; and in clear water, with careful handling, it is sometimes possible to land quite large fish. It is a nerve-racking business, though. Far better, I think, to use stronger line and, perhaps, delay fishing until the evening, when the light is fading. Chub will often take a fly fished on a strong cast then without fear. Four-pound breaking strain should be the minimum for the point. I often use six pound. The rod, too, should be more powerful. A reservoir or sea-trout rod, nine to ten feet in length, is more suitable than the brook rod I advised for

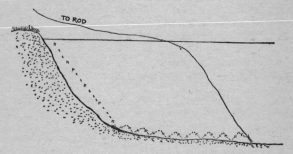

Figure 34. How to fish the sunken nymph

dace. Remember, the chub may head straight for the reeds and must be stopped. You cannot do this efficiently with tackle that is not suited to such a task.

The pattern of the fly is not too important, in my experience. Generations of angling writers have advised using big, bushy flies for chub. The Palmer flies and the big Sedge flies are useful, especially in the evening; but I have found that the smaller flies – even flies as small as those I have listed for dace – are often more killing during the day. The Coachman, Coch-y-bondhu and Alder are all fine chub flies. The Alder is perhaps the best of all during the summer.

I am now sure that the degree of light penetration considerably influences the chub's choice of fly. In general, if you use the smaller flies for the bright hours of the day and the larger ones at dusk, you will not err greatly.

Chub are not frequent risers, though, and it would be over-optimistic to expect to catch many with the fly. The most I ever caught in one session was three; and many times I have gone to the canal without catching one or even seeing a single rise. The calm, sunlit summer evenings are best. If there is a cold breeze on the water, the chances of catching chub with the dry-fly are low indeed.

Wet-fly and nymph fishing are always worth trying, of course. Bloody Butcher, Silver Butcher and Peter Ross are good patterns because they have a glint of silver on their bodies. I have not tried the Polystickle in canals, but I can see no logical reason why this lure should not also tempt chub. It is known to be deadly sometimes in rivers.

Other fish – such as perch, tench and bream – are rarely caught with flies. Perch will sometimes take wet-flies, particularly those with some glitter on their bodies. I once caught three within an hour while fishing for chub with a Silver Butcher on the point and a Peter Ross on a dropper; but there are better ways of catching perch from canals, and I would not normally advise any angler to pursue them deliberately with fly-fishing methods. They do rise to take flies from the surface, too, at times; but these are usually small shoal-perch which are not worth seeking. Big perch are more likely to succumb to a chub-sized wet-fly, or even to a salmon-fly. Game anglers sometimes catch them unwittingly while angling for sea-trout or salmon.

By way of contrast, rudd, when present in force, can often be caught in large numbers with dry-flies. When there is a glut of insect life on the water, a shoal of rudd will often work slowly upstream, taking insects at random, for a considerable length of time. I once followed a shoal that covered more than half a mile of water during the afternoon.

Rises may take place at any time of the day. In fact, it would be rare to sit by a canal with a large rudd population without seeing numerous rises during the summer months. In the evening, they often reach a peak – and this is probably the best time of all to catch a quantity of fish. Most of the patterns of fly I have mentioned for dace and roach will take them. Like most coarse fish, rudd do not display a high degree of selectivity. As long as the fly is small and carefully presented, the numbers of rudd rising will usually ensure that one of them will investigate the offering. Dry-flies are best for rudd, although they will take wet-flies and even small fly-spoons at times. The dry-fly is, however, a clear winner, in my experience.

As the season advances, the opportunity to capture fish with the fly diminishes; and once the really cold weather of winter begins to grip the countryside, the fly-rod can be laid aside. The months of June, July, August and September are the peak months. There are times during this period when the fly will catch more fish than a bait. It could even lure a trout or a grayling from those few canals that hold game fish.

Most anglers do not connect game fish with canals, and it is true that they are not commonly found in these waters unless it is a canal of exceptional purity – like the Driffield Canal, in Yorkshire. But even this fine water was once polluted. Now that it has been restored to something like its former high standard, many trout and grayling are taken from it every season. Baits such as maggots and red worms will tempt both these fish, but they are sought more often with the fly. Such well-known patterns as Black Gnat, Treacle Parkin, Tups Indispensible and John Storey, to mention a few, are all favoured flies. In Ireland, trout up to and over ten pounds in weight have been taken from the Cong Canal in County Mayo, mostly with spinners.

CHAPTER 17

Match Angling

Match angling in canals is a specialized form of angling. The matchman's aim is quite different from that of ordinary anglers. His object is to catch a higher weight of fish than his opponents within a limited time. He cannot prebait his swim; nor will he usually risk angling for big fish. He angles for the kind of fish which will enable him to build up a winning catch quickly. Time wasted may mean fish missed. Consequently, everything has to be speeded up. Casting, striking, retrieving the fish, groundbaiting – all must be done quickly and efficiently. A few ounces, or even drams, can swing the balance in his favour. To lose is not a disgrace. But to win or to be placed is an achievement. Reputations are at stake. Names can be made overnight. The competitive spirit is paramount.

It seems a great pity that all this effort so often reaps such a poor reward in terms of fish caught. Occasionally, an angler catches some good roach, bream, chub or tench, and the winning weight takes a spectacular upward leap. But more often than not, the weights returned are low and seldom give a true reflection of the quality of the canal's fishing. Some matches are won with a meagre two pounds or so of roach, or even with a mere ounce or two of small fish. One match fished on the Lancaster Canal, in which no less than 1,300 competitors took part, was won with less than four pounds of fish. In another match, fished in the Worcester Canal, the winner out of 164 competitors weighed in four pounds fourteen ounces of small roach. But one of the most fantastic match results of all must be the occasion when 200 sticklebacks earned an angler third place and £34 in prize money. The sticklebacks weighed six and a half ounces and were taken on a bloodworm fished on a size 22 hook.

Results of this kind are quite common when the catch is composed of small fish. Yet individual anglers often take hefty catches of fish, and sometimes large specimens, from these same waters when fishing alone. I can remember taking over thirty pounds of quality roach during an early morning session in the Alrewas Canal – a well-known Midlands match venue. This catch was witnessed by a bailiff and a few of the match anglers. Yet the match that was fished later in the day was won with only two pounds of small roach. Many anglers caught nothing.

It would be unwise to jump to conclusions about experiences such as this, though. Comparisons of the respective results in terms of fish caught can be misleading. I had the advantage of an early start in an undisturbed water. Also, I was fishing a swim I had been fishing for several days and I was using malt as bait, not maggots or bread.

Most match anglers are not prepared to take a chance with different baits but prefer those which have proved themselves over the years: maggots, casters and bread. Other factors often weigh heavily against them, too. They cannot choose their time or place, but must fish when and where the luck of the draw places them – quite often in most unfavourable conditions. To get the best from most canals, it is essential to be quiet and still. In this sense, the match angler commences at a disadvantage. The unavoidable amount of noise on the banks, and the fact that he is virtually rubbing shoulders with his fellow-competitors, creates adverse conditions which he must accept and strive to overcome. It is to his credit that he catches fish at all.

I do not fish in matches now; but when I was very young, I won a lot of matches by concentrating on gudgeon. Hordes of them then inhabited the local cut. I caught them by fishing a small blob of bread-paste hard on the bottom. The water was very clear and shallow, so I could see the paste easily. When it disappeared, I struck. Every match I won was with gudgeon caught in this manner.

It was juvenile stuff, of course – fished with enthusiasm, but without the knowledge that many years of hard experience in different waters can produce. Adult match anglers do not fish as lightheartedly. The sporting instinct is not dead but it is often submerged. Men engaged in competition are rivals. Only the most dedicated, most thorough and most ruthless reach the top. The keen match angler must be fit, his eyesight unimpaired. He cannot relax during long hours of concentration, staring at a tiny float. Faint-hearts who allow their attention to wander, or who give up because fish do not come to their nets quickly, seldom figure among the winners.

Most successful match anglers emphasize the value of having everything organized and getting in as much match practice on the water as possible. Between canals, there are often differences that repay study in the nature of the water and the fish. The match angler who knows the peculiarities of an individual water has a head start over his rivals. He begins fishing with more confidence, and he never gives up. Many matches have been won by anglers during the last hour, when less persistent competitors have given up and vacated their pegs. The successful match angler never admits defeat until the final whistle blows.

His tackle is carefully chosen, too. It has to be. Despite the old adage that a good workman never blames his tools, it is a fact that poorly designed and badly chosen tackle can seriously hamper a contestant's chances. Since he will seldom put his rod down, a light one is of enormous importance. An arm or wrist that is tired through holding a heavy rod will not react quickly enough at the vital moment, and fish may be missed. Most modern match rods weigh less than a pound.

The rod should also be long. Short rods are of little use for canal match fishing; so a rod which embodies both length and lightness is a highly desirable piece of equipment. In the past, match rods tended to be stereotyped in design, with bottom and middle sections of whole cane and only the tip of built-cane. Some were made of Spanish reed – light but inclined to be brittle. Today's match rod is a better all-round product. It is usually twelve to fifteen feet in length, of hollow built-cane or fibre-glass. Both materials are light, giving all-through action and better casting and striking action than the old type of rod. They can also be held for several hours without imposing undue strain on the wrist. Each angler has to find out, through experience, which rod is best suited to his own needs. Roach poles are little used, and it does not seem likely that match anglers are likely to abandon traditional favourites for these somewhat cumbersome pieces of equipment.

On the other hand, it must be admitted that the French style of angling, which frequently makes use of poles of up to twenty-five feet in length, does have certain advantages. Casting is eliminated. Instead, the bait is fished on a tight line, virtually under the rod-tip. This enables an angler to place his tackle accurately, and to hold it out wherever he wants it – which is a decided advantage when fishing the far bank or reaching out over intervening reeds. The rods – if they can properly be called by that name – look awkward and unwieldy when compared with the beautifully constructed English-style rods; but appearances are not important if their functional aspect is superior.

The French angler is usually equipped with several such rods of varying length with which he can fish any part of the canal merely by exchanging one for another. However prejudiced one might feel about this style, the results in terms of fish caught cannot be dismissed lightly.

A rate of three fish landed every minute is sometimes achieved by top-flight French anglers; and there can be no doubt that the long poles they use play a large part in the accomplishment of such fantastic results. The rigidity of the pole, which would normally lead to line failure, is offset by attaching a piece of elastic to a special fitting at the tip of the pole or to one of the rod rings. This acts as a shock-absorber when the strike is made; so very fine lines, as low as a half-pound breaking strain, can be used to catch the very small fish which are French anglers' very special forte.

English match anglers prefer to use reels – and these, too, have undergone a change since pre-war days, when the wooden centre-pin reel was much used. The fixed-spool reel has ousted this former favourite. Very few match anglers now use centre-pins for canal fishing. Casting with the fixed-spool reel is much simpler and quicker. Most match anglers carry at least two reels of this type and several spare spools of line, which are always ready for instant use. These are filled with lines ranging from three-quarters of a pound to two and a half pounds breaking strain. Such lines are deemed necessary to catch small fish in difficult conditions, where the thicker line could mean an empty net, and few match anglers use lines of greater strength. Hooking a large fish is an occupational hazard which the matchman must face up to and risk. If it does happen, he still has a chance of landing it if his swim is clear of snags and he handles the fish carefully. Unbelievable as it might sound, double-figure pike have been landed on lines of only one-and-a-half-pounds breaking strain.

As might be expected, the hooks used by canal match anglers are small. Size 18 is the most popular; but most anglers are prepared to use even smaller hooks if they think it necessary. Size 20, or even 22, is sometimes used to lure the small roach and perch that are the match angler's main quarry. The winner of one match, fished in the Lancaster Canal, used size 22 hook to three-quarters-of-a-pound line.

Eyed hooks are not popular for canal fishing, where even the weight of the hook may be of crucial importance when seeking the tiny fish that comprise the bulk of those caught in matches. Hooks ready-whipped to nylon are most popular since they are sharp, of fine wire, and are easily attached or removed by means of the loop with which this type of hook is completed. For quick and easy attachment, it is only necessary to form a similar loop at the end of the reel-line and push the loop on the hook through it. The hook goes through its own loop and is then carefully drawn tight. Bottoms of a foot or two in length are preferred to the yard bottom by most match anglers. The hook to a bottom measuring a foot is probably best of all, since the shotting can then be mainly confined to the reel-line and hook changes can be made without reshotting. It saves time – and time is very valuable to the match angler (Fig 35).

HOOK TO NYLON   REEL-LINE

Figure 35. Method of attaching hook link to reel-line

Spade-end hooks are second in the popularity stakes, and understandably so. They are cheap, and the nimble-fingered match angler can whip his own hooks direct to the line. Spade-ends are every bit as good as ready-whipped hooks if they are tied carefully.

Many anglers throw their hooks away after use. This seems a wise policy. Hooks are cheap. It would be false economy to preserve a tiny hook that had become blunted or distorted through constant use.

The French carry the small-hook fetish to an extreme which few English match anglers would seek to emulate. Hooks of size 28 or even less cause no raised eyebrows in France, especially when the much-favoured bloodworm is being used as bait. A hook of this size might seem fantastically small; but when one considers the smallness of the bait and then ponders on the fact that a French angler once landed two hundred and thirty fish in one and half hours while using such a hook and bait, then one must begin to feel healthy respect rather than surprise or derision.

The floats used by match anglers are numerous and varied. Tiny quills and self-cockers, in many different sizes and colours, are popular. So are small antenna floats. Some match anglers number their floats carefully with the amount of shot each one will carry, so that it can be discerned at a glance. The popularity of the various floats waxes and wanes. Keen eyes and ears glean scraps of information about the methods and tackle used by current winners. Perhaps a new float has been designed. Maybe a different method or bait has been used. Match anglers are ever alert to any news that might filter through on the grapevine. It is difficult for any angler to keep a secret for long.

Benny Ashurst's success in canal matches has naturally focused attention on his tackle. His 'stick float', with its buoyant tip and heavy cane base, has made a big impact. The float cocks slowly, with an action described by its innovator as 'pendulum'. The buoyant tip holds the float at surface level while the heavier base sinks slowly in an arc. For canal fishing in a slow-sinking style one BB shot is placed directly under the float, and a dust shot about a foot from the hook. This float is normally attached to the line by both rings.

In the Midlands, the tiny self-cocker or the quill is often preferred. This is frequently shotted so that the weight will slightly sink the float when the bait is fully sunk. If this does not happen, it is assumed that a fish has taken the bait. The last shot is often placed only an inch or so from the hook for better bite registration (Fig 36). It can be a deadly method of taking small fish with bread-baits and small maggots.

By way of contrast, French match anglers often prefer small antenna floats or floats made from balsa wood or peacock quills. The float is usually fished on a tight line, beneath the rod-tip, and is generally attached by both rings. The French call this style *la pêche à la ligne*.

One could easily draw comparisons between this style and the roach-pole techniques of the old-style Thames angler – a style that seems to have fallen into disrepute now but which was often used, in my younger days, by small boys who had to make do with one-piece cane poles because they could not afford anything else. It looks clumsy, but it can be very effective.

The French often use a different type of lead weight from that used in England. Instead of a split shot, the French angler uses a streamlined lead which is threaded onto the line and prevented from sliding onto the hook by means of a dust shot. When it is desired to get the bait down quickly, the last shot is attached to the line approximately three inches from the hook. This arrangement is reputed to give a smoother entry of the bait into the water; to get it down nearer to the bottom more quickly; and to lessen resistance when the fish takes the bait, because the line slips easily through the lead (Fig 37).

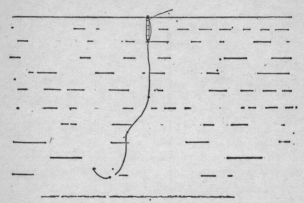

Figure 36. Slow-sinking style with 'overloaded' self-cocker

Anglers might like to consider an idea of mine which I have often put to practical use when using a similar style of fishing. It is really a variation on the slow-sinking style I described for roach fishing. First, the float is threaded on the line, then the smallest of swivels, and finally a rubber stop is tied a few inches from the hook. Any further weight that is needed, to give either a slow-sinking or quick-sinking effect, can be attached to a small nylon link which is tied to the other eye of the swivel. The rubber stop is better than a split shot, in my opinion. It performs the same function but does not damage or weaken the line. The line runs through the swivel, which acts as a weight as well, and achieves precisely the same effect as the French rig (Fig 38).

Canal match anglers in England still use the traditional

'fine and far off' style. Far-bank fishing is almost standard practice in many canals, and few anglers deviate from this. The reason is not difficult to define. When anglers are present in large numbers, in plain view of the fish, it is not surprising that most of the fish should retire to the deeper water under the far bank or in the boat-road. Noise on the bank is an unavoidable obstacle to success in canals, and the match angler must adjust his tactics to offset this. There is rarely anything to be gained from fishing the near bank; but there is everything to be gained from fishing the bait where the fish are most likely to be.

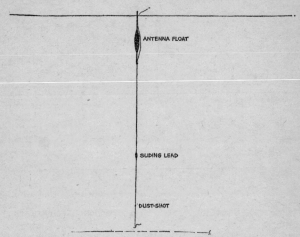

Figure 37. French style with sliding lead weight

When using this style, it is generally accepted that it is most effective as long as the bait is kept falling through the water, and that it is usually bad policy to leave the float in the water when it is fully sunk. When that happens, the tackle is retrieved and recast. The aim is to pick up fish that are lying in the higher stratas of water, so the tackle should be adjusted and shotted to achieve this end. The angler must always be working for his fish – not waiting for them to find his bait. It is not surprising therefore that most of the fish caught are small.

This is not necessarily true in all cases, though. Sometimes the bigger fish do move in. Roach of over a pound in weight, and some of over two pounds, are sometimes caught. Bream and tench are numbered among the smaller fish, too, occasionally – more often in canals where they are numerous. It may surprise some to learn that such fish will sometimes move up through the water to take a slowly sinking bait, but such experiences are not as rare as might be expected.

On some occasions, the match angler may find that few if any of these fish can be taken 'on the drop'; so he must start to get his bait down deeper to catch the gudgeon, bream or odd tench that might be lurking there. Some canals hold quite large stocks of these fish; and, often, match anglers who know this make a deliberate decision to go after them. Many matches have been won in recent years with bream. In particular, the Worcester Canal and the Trent and Mersey Canal, at Stone, have provided many winning catches in which bream predominated. These bream have sometimes fallen to such unusual baits as hemp seed; but maggots and worms have accounted for most of them.

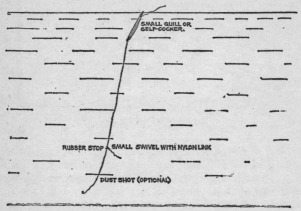

Figure 38. The author's favourite fine-line tackle

The basic tackle set-up of a fine line and small hook is not abandoned when bream are the quarry. Few match anglers would risk changing to a heavier tackle and a larger hook. Under normal conditions of clear water, this seems a wise decision. Both bream and tench can be very finicky. To fish a small bait such as a maggot or a caster on a large hook and a stronger line could be a fatal mistake. A total and drastic change of method and tackle is necessary if any change has to be made at all. Any form of compromise would be unsatisfactory and could mean many missed fish. The match angler copes by altering his depth and shotting so that the bait sinks more quickly and stays on or near the bottom.

The baits used by match anglers vary from maggots, bread and casters to the occasional use of one of the lesser-known baits that I have referred to. Maggots are clear favourites, and understandably so since every known species of fish will take them. Ordinary shop-bought maggots will not suffice for some match anglers, though. They breed their own 'specials', and guard their secret processes carefully. The yellow Annato maggots are firm favourites. Squats and pinkies are also freely used, mainly as feeders.

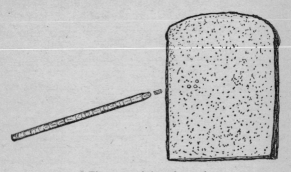

Figure 39. A bread-punch

Next in popularity is bread, which is mostly used in very small pieces of flake. Crust and paste are not widely used at all now. In some areas, bread is still supreme. Skilled exponents in the art of the slow-sinking style sometimes build up large catches of small fish with this bait. Quite often, a bread-punch is used to extract fragments of bread from a cut loaf. The punch is merely a metal tube with a sharp cutting edge, approximately one-eighth of an inch in diameter. This produces small pieces of bread, of uniform size, which are untouched by hand (Fig 39). Once the bread is extracted from the slice, the hook is inserted into the narrow slit at the edge of the punch to bring out the bread.

The smallness of the bait makes small hooks and fine tackle a necessity. Lines as low as three-quarters-of-a-pound breaking strain, coupled with a size 20 hook, is often used to take small roach with a bait that sinks very slowly through the clear water. A tiny float is also used. One which can be shotted to show only a fraction of an inch of its tip when weighted with a few dust shot is preferred. In the hands of a skilled user, this is deadly for small roach and adds considerably to the speed and efficiency of mechanical tasks like baiting the hook and striking. The tiny roach which are so often caught with this method are extracted in a straightforward no-nonsense style which lifts the fish from the water and into the angler's lap in the minimum of time. Nets are superfluous. Rods are often tip-actioned only.

The bait currently in fashion is undoubtedly the caster. Many match anglers claim that it is superior to maggots. Very rarely is it used on the surface or on the bottom, as I have described. The usual style is similar to that used with the bread bait: a slow-sinking across-the-canal style. The true caster, which has been carefully separated from the floaters, does not need the addition of any weight in normal conditions. Possibly, this accounts in some measure for its outstanding success as a bait for match fishing. Better roach are often caught with casters, and both bream and chub will take them too.

Other baits, such as cheese and the seed-baits, are rarely used. Match anglers claim that it usually takes too long to get the fish interested in them and they cannot afford to waste valuable time. There is a lot of truth in this, but I would except waters where these baits are used frequently. In my experience, it is often possible to catch roach quickly from such waters – sometimes with the very first cast. Roach caught with these baits are usually bigger than those caught with other baits.

The only other bait of real significance is the controversial bloodworm. This is the tiny larva of the Chironomids, which has a characteristic red colour – hence its name. It is gathered in fine nets from mud-bottomed environments, and it is said to be a deadly bait for small fish of all kinds. French anglers use it frequently. In England, Wigan is reputed to be the home of the expert bloodworm angler.

Such a tiny bait demands a small hook and delicate presentation. The bloodworm is normally mounted on a size 20 or 22 hook to three-quarters-of-a-pound line. The float, usually a small cane-and-balsa-wood type, carries a few dust shot which are arranged on the cast to give the usual slow-sinking effect. Large catches of small fish are often made with this bait. As a result, it has sometimes been banned on the grounds that it gives its users an unfair advantage.

In France, the bloodworm is a favourite bait but by no means the only one. Hemp seed, wheat, flies, ants, congealed blood, shrimps, and – believe it or not – the eyes of a perch are all used. Coloured beads are popular too – especially red ones, because of the similarity in colouring to the bloodworm. Various pastes blended from potatoes, hard-boiled egg yolks, crushed biscuits, hemp seed and honey are manufactured and bought by the French angler in search of a magic bait. It is debatable whether these additives improve the attractive qualities of plain paste, but the French angler is willing to give them all a trial.

Groundbaiting is an essential part of the match angler's technique. It is prepared thoroughly, and is of such a consistency that it will closely match the style of angling used. The groundbait for roach is usually composed of fine particles of baked, crushed bread mixed, perhaps, with a fine meal such as sausage-rusk. This is soaked and squeezed out into small balls which disintegrate upon impact with the water. Most match anglers are of the opinion that this should be used on the basis of 'a little and often'. The aim is to concentrate the small roach into a tight area and get them feeding on the slowly sinking bait that will be used in conjunction with this type of groundbait. Small maggots (pinkies) are often mixed in with the groundbait.

A heavier type of groundbait which will sink more quickly is preferred when bream are the quarry. It is often said that no angler can carry enough groundbait for bream; but in canal match fishing, it must not be overdone. Too much might scare off the shoal; 'a little and often' is a better and wiser tactic. Small balls, about the size of a hen's egg, made heavier by the addition of more water, and perhaps a heavier meal, like wheatmeal, are not as likely to scare the bream as several handfuls dropping like bombs into the swim.

In match-fishing circles, it is almost inevitable that there should be talk of alleged preference on the part of the fish for special-flavoured groundbaits, or for those with some colour in them. Gimmicks, rumours and speculations are always more potent and more commonplace in circles where the originator's aim might be sincere but might equally be an attempt to mislead or confuse the opposition. Personally. I doubt whether additives of any kind have any significant effect on the feeding habits of the fish, unless they have some relationship to the hook-bait – as when flaked maize or spent grains are used as additional groundbait when seed-bait fishing.

Some anglers, including many French specialists, might differ strongly about such a conclusion. It is said that at least one hundred forms of commercially manufactured groundbait can be bought in France, all of which are reputed to have special fish-attracting properties; and this figure does not include the privately concocted mixtures which individual anglers blend themselves.

In England, the number of proprietary groundbaits that can be bought is much smaller. Most match anglers prefer to make up their own; but very few would ever enter a match without any groundbait at all. Quite probably, in view of the match angler's preoccupation with small fish, this decision is a wise one. Yet matches have been won in rivers by anglers fishing without groundbait – and quite often using a bigger bait than that normally used.

Canal fishing is not like river fishing, of course; and match fishing is different from pleasure fishing. But I think that if we could dispense once and for all with the idea that match angling in canals must necessarily mean angling for small fish, and if match rules could be altered to allow each angler far more space than he enjoys now, and if boat traffic could be halted – at least for the duration of the match – then perhaps match weights would take a more consistent upward leap.

The odds against catching big fish in a match are long, I know. Yet the fish are there to be caught in many canals; that much is beyond dispute. And in many canals there are roach of up to and over two pounds in weight; also big bream, tench and chub. The real problem is knowing when it would pay to risk fishing for them. That is the matchman's dilemma.

CHAPTER 18

Maintenance of Canals

Policy

It is regrettable, from the angler's point of view, that many canals that were once fine fisheries have either been abandoned or filled in. Yet it would be pointless now to speculate about what might have been. The main purpose for which canals were built – that of providing a means of transporting goods cheaply – no longer seems a valid reason for keeping them open. Fast trains and motorized transport have taken over this role and are not likely to be displaced. As a result, many hundreds of miles of canals have fallen into disuse and neglect. The only remaining reason for keeping them open seems to be their value as a means of recreation for boating enthusiasts and anglers.

Under the present scheme approximately 1,400 miles of canal waterways – comprising, 1,100 locks and 270 aqueducts – are being retained for pleasure cruising and angling. The remainder are closed, but not necessarily doomed. The door has been left open for interested parties to undertake voluntary restoration work, provided that they are prepared to finance it themselves. Some angling clubs have undertaken such work and carried it through to a successful conclusion. The Stratford-on-Avon Canal was taken over by the National Trust, and volunteer workers cleaned out the canal and performed repair work on the locks.

In most cases, though, restoration work has been carried out by angling clubs or devoted enthusiasts like members of the Inland Waterways Association. The expenses incurred can be high, but it is possible to recoup at least part of these by increased sales of angling licences and, perhaps, by increased charges. Many anglers who would not pay to fish in a neglected water are prepared to pay once it has been cleared.

As an indication of what can be done, a small angling club raised the £200 they needed to clear out a one-and-a-half-mile stretch of the Chesterfield Canal from club members' contributions of only sixpence a week. Afterwards, the club secretary expressed an opinion that more stretches of canal could be saved if other clubs showed similar enthusiasm, because it is cheaper to restore a canal than to fill it in. A similar opinion was expressed about the decaying Pocklington Canal. Officials of the local angling club and the Inland Waterways Association estimated a cost of only £40,000 to restore the canal, while the Transport Commission's estimate for compensation and filling in came to £70,000. It is worth noting that local authorities might contribute something towards the cost of restoration if they consider the preservation of the local canal essential to the development of local amenities.

Naturally, most anglers would like to retain every fishable yard of canal; but such an idea seems impossible to attain. When the Waterways Board took over the canals, in 1963, they inherited a deficit of £6,000,000. The Government revealed that it was not prepared to bear the total cost of keeping open the canals but was prepared to grant an annual reducing subsidy towards their upkeep. The implication that the Waterways Board was expected to become self-sufficient was quite clear. Anglers contribute very little towards the total revenue, as can be seen quite clearly from a comparison of the income derived by the Board from various sources. In 1966, for instance, the sale of water brought in £663,739. Boating yielded £106,386. The return from the sale of fishing rights was only £22,515. Anglers are therefore in the unfortunate position of being a minority group with little bargaining power.

The number of people using the canals for boating is difficult to assess. According to an estimate for 1966–7 given in the publication *Leisure and Waterways*, 6,000 powered boats and 2,800 unpowered boats use the canals. If we assume that each of these boats would carry a minimum of two people, then the number of people using the canals for boating must be at least 18,000. The actual figure is probably much higher – nearer to 30,000. By way of comparison, the number of anglers using canals on any average Sunday is often in excess of 24,000. On one wet Sunday, 27,275 anglers were fishing. These figures only indicate the numbers of anglers fishing on a given day. Assuming that there are now well over 3,000,000 anglers in Britain, many of whom use the canals frequently from June until the following March, then it is obvious that the number of anglers fishing in canals throughout the season must be much higher than those using them for boating. It is equally obvious that the revenue from canal angling is ridiculously small in relationship to the number of anglers fishing.

There is, unfortunately, a clash of interests between boating enthusiasts and anglers. Boats disturb the water and are often resented by anglers. It is difficult to see how the rival interests can be reconciled. The only aim they seem to have in common is the preservation of the canals. But this, at least, gives them a basis for cooperation.

At the moment, boating enthusiasts might feel that they have a greater right to use the canals than anglers if only because their financial contribution is greater. It seems obvious that an increase in the cost of canal angling licences must be considered if anglers are to compete on anything like equal terms with boat users. In return, anglers could legitimately expect that everything possible would be done to improve the quality of the fishing in canals, where necessary, and that as many miles of canals as was financially possible would be kept open for angling. It would also help if boat traffic could be restricted to certain hours of the day – say, between 9 AM and 7 PM – and banned entirely for the duration of a fishing match. Such a restriction might not be popular with boat users, but it would be welcomed by anglers – particularly match anglers. Discussions and decisions upon policy could be made at a local level by representatives of all interested parties. The aim must be cooperation – not division and antagonism.

Reed-clearance

This is another problem about which there is considerable dissension. Most canals are subjected to periodic reed-cutting operations, usually by a mechanical cutter which removes all visible reed but leaves the roots intact. The majority of anglers prefer reed-free waters to fish in and are pleased when the cutter has cleared out the reeds. I do not share this view at all. Reeds play a very important part in the ecology of any water. They are the habitat of countless tiny organisms upon which fish feed. They provide shelter for the fish – and for the angler, if he has the wit to use them for this purpose. They also provide much of the life-giving oxygen without which fish die. Remembering this, it seems to me that the wholesale removal of all reeds must be regarded as an act of the utmost folly.

Some reeds must be removed periodically to keep a canal open for navigation and to keep it in a fishable condition; but I am sure that the interests of the angler would be best served by partial and thoughtful clearance rather than the wholesale clearance that is carried out by so many river boards. I suggest that it would be sufficient to keep open a broad channel down the boat-road and, perhaps, clear areas adjacent to the bank at intervals of twenty yards or so. The canal would then be navigable and fishable while yet retaining a plentiful supply of reeds that are essential to the life of the myriads of different organisms that inhabit a healthy water. The canal would also be more attractive visually. A water stripped of its natural fauna, and sometimes of much of its bankside growth too, might be easier to fish, but it has also lost much of its natural appeal, is less pleasing to the eye and has probably been rendered deficient in many different organisms upon which fish feed.

In extreme cases, a deterioration in the quality of the fishing can result from such wholesale clearances, especially when the operations are combined with dredging and, possibly, some form of pollution. Singly or in concert, these activities often have an adverse effect that is more dangerous than it might seem since the total effect is hidden from the human eye – often remaining unobserved and unrealized until the damage has progressed to that stage where only it becomes apparent from the poor returns of quality fish. A more thoughtful approach to reed-clearance is needed, I am sure. The angler has nothing to lose but everything to gain from a new approach, and he should press for it with his club or whichever local authority is responsible for the maintenance of his canal.

Restocking

No aspect of fishery management is so fraught with danger, so influenced by misconceptions, and so little understood as this one.* In many cases, a canal has only to fish badly for a

* Readers are advised to consult works such as *The Management of Coarse Fishing Waters* by Eric Birch; *Life in Lakes and Rivers* by Macan and Worthington; *Freshwater Ecology* by T.T. Macan; and similar works, for authoritative information.

while for pressure to be put on a club secretary to 'improve' the water by restocking. Very rarely is expert advice sought; and few, if any, anglers ever give much thought to the possible consequences of such an action. It is sufficient that the fishing does not live up to their expectations. Therefore, it is reasoned, it must be because there are not enough fish in the water. The only obvious solution is to put more in.

One might wish that the solution to a problem was always as simple and uncomplicated as this. As a short-term measure, extensive restocking can *appear* to be beneficial. The new stocks of fish may never have seen a baited hook before. Their introduction will undoubtedly increase the competition for available food. Not surprisingly, since more fish will be actively seeking food, they will be easier to catch. In extreme cases, the water might become overpopulated and overstocked within a very short space of time. The ultimate result of such a situation can never be to the angler's benefit. Waters that are overpopulated seldom produce big fish. Most fish remain small, stunted and ridiculously easy to catch. So, far from being improved, a water that is restocked without it first being determined whether it can sustain the additional stocks might actually deteriorate. The improvement manifested by increased catches may be largely illusory. The long-term effects of ill-advised restocking can be disastrous.

What is very often wrong is that those responsible seldom give sufficient thought to why the canal is fishing badly. The fish may possibly have grown wary of or sickened by normal baits through over-fishing. Disease, or some form of pollution, might also be partly responsible. Another reason could be that the canal is so well-endowed with natural food that the fish are not inclined to take baits readily. Waters of this type generally hold many large fish – sometimes, as in the case of the Macclesfield Canal, outstanding specimen fish. These can sometimes be observed. If not, a limited spell of electro-fishing or netting would reveal whether the water holds good fish. And if these operations show a healthy water with a large head of big fish, those responsible should ask themselves whether it would be wise to interfere with existing stocks. Waters that breed big fish are not common. It would seem extremely foolish to risk disturbing the delicate balance of life in the water by the wholesale introduction of new stocks. Possibly no disastrous results of restocking would become immediately apparent; but a change, however slight, in the established pattern of life in the water would be inevitable. The new fish would undoubtedly compete for available food. They could also introduce disease and, in many little-understood ways, ruin what was once an excellent fishery.

If examination revealed that a water was overpopulated and deficient in natural food supplies, however, then steps could be taken to rectify the matter. The removal of large numbers of fish could be considered as a first step. In the normal course of events, several different species of fish inhabit a canal. It is possible that some species would reveal quite good growth rates while others would be poor. And certain species, such as roach, might be numerically superior to all the other species combined and yet reveal poor growth rates. If this were so, it might seem a wise policy to reduce the roach population. This action might have beneficial results; but then again, it might not. If other fish such as bream and rudd are competing intensively for the same type of food as the roach, a total reduction of stocks of these particular species might be better.

If there are few or no predators in the water in the form of pike and perch, then the introduction of these two species could also be considered. In their infancy, perch compete with other species for the minute organisms that inhabit these waters; but as they grow older, they turn increasingly to feeding off other fish. They, in turn, are preyed upon by pike. So it is possible that the introduction of one or both of these species would improve rather than harm the water. But if the existing species attain good sizes in the absence of the predators, it would not be wise to introduce them. Each water is individual. To introduce new species is a step that should not be taken without careful examination and consideration of existing stocks.

The causes of poor growth in fish cannot always be attributed to overcrowding alone, though. If the water is lacking in essential nutrients, then no amount of restocking is likely to bring about any dramatic improvement. In fact, it could truthfully be said that a water deficient in nutrient salts cannot possibly support a large and healthy fish population. Alkaline waters produce a more prolific reed-growth which, in turn, results in a higher density of animal life for the fish to feed on. They also usually produce a prolific population of mulluscs; and, in my experience, a water that is rich in crustacea is often a very good water, yielding a high proportion of big fish. It will also probably hold uncountable numbers of other forms of life, ranging from the minute sponge-like organisms that attach themselves to stones to such forms of life as snails, shrimps, beetles, water-skaters and crayfish, together with the nymphs and larvae of various flies and insects that live in or around the water. Damsel-flies, dragonflies and innumerable quantities of gnats and midges can be seen on the waters of most canals during the summer. If close examination reveals that most if not all of these forms of life are absent from a water, then there must be a strong suspicion that all is not well. Pollution may be the cause.

Pollution

Canals have not suffered from pollution to the same degree that many of our rivers have; but one sees that it is inevitable that some pollution should occur when one considers the number of possible sources. These can be broadly categorized as pollution from airborne gases, from drainage systems connected to farmlands and various industrial establishments, and from boats.

The amount of pollution resulting from airborne gases is probably very small and is more likely to occur in canals that flow through highly industrial areas. The effect on fish of dissolved gases such as sulphur dioxide is difficult to define. In isolation, the effect might be negligible in view of the small amount of gas that would be in the water. High concentrations of this gas are, of course, lethal to man as well as fish. So is carbon monoxide – large quantities of which, in the form of exhaust fumes, are expelled into the atmosphere every day. What the long-term, cumulative effect of these gases is on our waterways is not known; but it might well be more significant than is generally thought.

There can be no doubt, though, that the most serious form of pollution is that which results from the discharge of polluted matter into the water. This can be as serious and as devastating to fish-life in a canal as it is in a river. The case of the Manchester Ship Canal demonstrates emphatically how damaging such pollution can be. This canal was described in Parliament as 'one of the largest navigable sewers in the world' – a statement which subsequently led to steps being take to improve the quality of the effluents being discharged into it. But this water is still far below the standard of purity that should be regarded as essential in a canal.

Another serious case of pollution – from a fractured sewer in a stretch of the St Helen's Canal, at Newton-le-Willows, Lancashire – resulted in the death of thousands of fish, including roach of up to two and a half pounds in weight. Even sticklebacks died. The destruction of fish-life in this stretch was catastrophic and swift. According to reports, the canal was normal one day and covered with dead and dying fish the next day.

In another case, a discharge by the National Coal Board into the Daerne and Dove Canal resulted in a large number of fish dying. Cases of oil pollution and pollution from agricultural effluent of various kinds have also been reported.

Pollution from the discharge of sewage undoubtedly increases during the summer, when boat traffic is at its peak. It is encouraging to learn that disposal points are being established. And it is to be hoped that not only will their numbers be increased but that also all boat-users will be encouraged to use them. The discharge of sewage into any water must be detrimental; and it is particularly dangerous during the summer, when the temperature is high and the water at a low level.

I think it should be emphasized that pollution does not necessarily result in the immediate loss of fish life. Pollution can be a slow, gradual process; and it is more dangerous then because its effects do not become apparent until the concentrations of poisonous matter become lethal and the fish begin to appear sick or begin to die.

Pollution can also affect fish-life by destroying or reducing those forms of life upon which fish feed. In 1968, a deterioration in the quality of the fishing in Midlands canals was thought to be due to a virus transmitted by birds. The virus caused the fish to go blind. It is possible, though, that other factors were responsible for bringing about this affliction. In her far-sighted book *Silent Spring*, Rachel Carson revealed that land-spraying with DDT, which eventually found its way into a nearby watercourse, not only resulted in the death of many fish but also induced symptoms of blindness among the survivors. There is evidence enough here, I feel, to suspect that the widespread use of insecticides on farmlands adjoining canals may contribute to the deterioration of a water and its fish. It is now known that fish can absorb and accumulate lethal concentrations of chemicals commonly used for pest prevention. It is my opinion that the laws regarding the use of insecticides are far too lax, and that not enough is known about the long-term effects insecticides can have on water, fish and, indirectly, the bird- and animal-life that frequents the waterside. According to the report of the Nature Conservancy (1963), residues of organo-chlorines are high in fish-eating species of birds such as herons and grebes – a fact which leaves little doubt that these poisons are infecting our waterways.

The enemies of fish-, bird- and animal-life have increased tremendously during the last decade. Fifty years ago, horses were used to pull barges along the canals – and, indeed, continued to do so until after the 1939–45 war. Powered boats were practically unknown, as were the present range of insecticides. And anglers normally kept their fish, thus contributing in a small way to the pruning of fish stocks.

All of this has changed. Anglers return their fish. Pollution from oil, petrol, sewage and chemicals is a constant danger. This is clearly a matter of national concern. Pure water is essential not only to fish but also to human beings. Fortunately, there are signs that the public is at last becoming aware of the nature and extent of the evil of pollution and that the Government is beginning to take more active steps to eliminate this scourge. This is one policy that I feel must be pursued with determination until all sources of pollution have finally been eliminated. Nothing less should suffice.

APPENDIX

The Common Fish of Britain's Canals

Roach *(Rutilus rutilus)*

Roach are quite the most numerous of all canal fish. The majority of canals hold thousands of them. Their average weight is probably from four to six ounces, but some have been caught of up to and over three pounds. Their colouring makes them distinctive and easy to recognize. The flanks are brilliant silver, sometimes flushed with pale gold but more commonly with a steely blue sheen. The back is green-blue. The anal and pelvic fins are coral and the other fins are usually a pale, watery brown. The edge of the dorsal fin is concave, and it has from nine to eleven branched rays. The mouth does not contain any teeth. These are arranged in the lower part of the throat and are called pharyngeal teeth. The lower lip recedes slightly from the upper one. The scale count, taken along the lateral line, is usually from forty to forty-six.

Roach are shoal fish, especially in their infancy, and are largely vegetarian in their feeding habits, eating considerable amounts of filamentous reeds and algae, as well as the minute organisms which feed upon the algae. Later in life, they graduate to more substantial food in the form of nymphs, caddis and small molluscs. Like most fish, they must feed largely upon that food which is available. Thus, at one stage of the season they may feed more upon one kind of food than another, graduating to each in turn as they become more plentiful. Roach in one canal may have quite different feeding habits from those in another, mainly because of the difference in the ecology of various canals. Some have a plentiful supply of natural foods. Others are deficient; and in these canals the roach may tend to be small and easy to catch. Roach in canals that are rich in fauna and natural foods will usually be of a much higher average size and weight, but they will be more difficult to catch.

Rudd *(Scardinius erythrophthalmus)*

These handsome fish are remarkably similar to roach in size and shape. In fact, they are often confused with roach in Ireland, where they are very common and roach are very scarce. In England, they are neither as widespread nor as common as roach, but they are found in some canals. They are handsome fish, with a back of greenish colour, flanks tarnished silver and brilliant scarlet fins. This vivid colouring alone is sufficient to distinguish them from roach, but there are other distinguishing characteristics. The lower lip juts out slightly beyond the upper one. The dorsal fin has from eight to ten branched rays and is set farther back than that of the roach. The anal fin has from ten to thirteen branched rays. The scale count along the lateral line is from thirty-nine to forty-four. Like roach, they have pharyngeal teeth only, and they feed mainly on the same kind of foods. They are, however, more inclined to take food from the surface and can often be seen there, feeding off various insects and their nymphs. They are shoal fish, averaging around a half a pound in weight in most canals; but they can grow to even larger sizes than roach. A two-pound rudd is an outstanding canal fish, though, by any standards.

Bream *(Abramis brama)*

There should be no possibility of confusion between this species and the previous two. Even in infancy, bream are altogether less striking in appearance: pale, silver-coloured fish, with fins of an undistinguished neutral colour. They are also deeper in the body, narrower across the back, and often very slimy. Adult bream grow to a much larger average size than either rudd or roach. A two-pound bream is a good average-sized fish; but specimens of up to six pounds and more in weight have been taken from some canals. Small bream – or 'skimmers', as they are sometimes called – are often very numerous.

Like roach and rudd, bream have pharyngeal teeth only. The scale count along the lateral line is usually between forty-nine and fifty-seven. The dorsal fin has from eight to ten branched rays; and the anal fin has from twenty-three to twenty-nine. Bream are largely bottom feeders, seeking out nymphs, bloodworms and small crustacea in the mud and silt.

They are widely distributed, though not seen or caught as frequently as the more common roach.

Chub *(Squalus cephalus)*

Chub are sometimes confused with roach. But to the practised eye, the differences between them are so obvious that it is difficult to understand why there should ever be any confusion. In appearance, chub are bigger, longer and thicker through the back than roach; and they have a characteristic blunt head, and thick whitish lips. Their colouring is usually dark greenish-brown along the back. The flanks are from dull gold to bronze as opposed to the brilliant silver one associated with roach. Variations in colouring do occur; but only very rarely are chub bright silver. Their fins are usually a dull, neutral colour too – with the exception of the belly fins, which are often pink or coral. The dorsal fin and the anal fin are both *convex* – an important means of identification when distinguishing small chub from dace.

Chub also have a very powerful set of pharyngeal teeth. These can seriously damage an unwary finger thrust down a chub's throat. They have from forty-two to forty-nine scales along the lateral line, and from seven to nine branched rays in the anal and dorsal fins. They are not often found in large shoals, but in small groups of varying sizes. They feed on a varied assortment of plant- and animal-life, but are more predatory than the other fish. They feed ravenously on minnows and the fry of other fish, and have even been observed to eat small rodents such as voles. They reach a good average weight from three to four pounds, but specimens of from five to six pounds have been taken from some canals.

Dace *(Leuciscus leuciscus)*

Similar to chub in appearance but much smaller and more silvery in colour, dace have a more sharply pointed head. The dorsal and anal fins are *concave* – more noticeably the anal fin – and are of an undistinguished neutral colour. There are from forty-seven to fifty-four scales along the lateral line. The dorsal fin has seven or eight branched rays; the anal fin has from seven to nine.

Dace are essentially shoal fish and are seldom found alone. They feed extensively on minute organisms, notably the larvae and the flies of the Chironomids. An eight-ounce dace could be accounted an outstanding fish for a canal. The average size is much smaller, probably weighing two or three ounces. Like chub, dace are river fish that have adapted themselves to a different environment quite successfully.

Tench (*Tinca tinca*)

There can be no mistaking tench. They are smooth, finely scaled fish, dark brown or greenish in colour. The eyes are red, and there is a small barbule at each corner of the mouth. The fins are all rounded; the tail is thick and strong. The dorsal fin has eight or nine branched rays; the anal fin has from six to eight. Because they are so small, there are an exceptional number of scales along the lateral line – usually between ninety-nine and one hundred and twenty.

Tench are almost exclusively bottom feeders, but they can sometimes be seen browsing among the reeds, where they love to bury themselves. They eat a wide range of organisms, ranging from bloodworms to molluscs.

Some canals hold a lot of tench, others very few. The size range varies from very small, where the fish are stunted, to large fish weighing four, five or even six pounds. A two-pound canal tench could be accounted a good fish.

Perch (*Perca fluviatilis*)

There can be no more easily distinguished fish than perch. The back is usually olive or bottle-green, merging to a lighter green on the flanks, and finally to a milky-white underbelly. They are also distinguished by several darker-coloured bars running vertically down each flank. There are usually six of these, giving perch a characteristic striped appearance. The head is pointed, the mouth large, and the back humped. There are two dorsal fins, both prickly with spikes. The gills are spiny too, and they can inflict a sharp wound on the unwary hand. The skin of perch is rough to the touch and not slimy. The mouth contains slanting teeth. In fact, perch look and are predators in every sense of the word. They feed extensively on the fry of other fish, and even on their own young.

In most canals, perch are numerous; but only the small ones bite readily. The larger fish are more difficult to tempt. A perch weighing half a pound is a fair, average size for a canal. Much larger fish are sometimes caught from the best waters. Specimens of well over three pounds in weight have been recorded.

Pike *(Esox lucius)*

By far the largest of all canal fish, pike grow up to and over twenty pounds in weight. Fish weighing between three and seven pounds are common in many canals. Like perch, they are predators – fish-eaters. Their colouring is designed for camouflage. The dappled yellow-green colour enables them to merge with reeds, where they lie in ambush to seize an unwary fish that passes. The head is elongated, and the jaw is thin, bony and aggressive-looking. The eyes, unlike those of other fish, focus forwards from the front of the head. Pike are capable of quick bursts of speed, and they will actively hunt down their prey when hungry.

Small pike, also known as 'jacks', feed mainly upon insects at first, and then upon small fry and minnows. The larger fish eat these small fish, too, but will often take much bigger fish. A two-pound roach or bream is consumed with ease. The smaller pike are not immune from attack by adult pike. They are immensely strong fish. Very large pike are usually females.

Eels *(Anguilla anguilla)*

No other canal fish remotely resembles these. In appearance, they are more like snakes than fish. The back is dark, usually olive green in colour. The belly is usually white or yellow. The head is pointed. The eyes are small, and the teeth are numerous and sharp.

Eels will eat almost anything, and probably clean up most of the dead fish that can be seen in canals. They often lie hidden in some hole or crevice, or in a thick bed of reeds, until they are hungry. They feed most freely at night – but not exclusively then, as was once supposed. Unlike most other fish, they migrate to sea to spawn. Their average weight is around one or two pounds. Larger specimens of up to five pounds or more are not uncommon, though.

SMALL FISH

Gudgeon *(Gobio gobio)*

The most important of small fish are gudgeon – bottom-feeding fish with the characteristic down-turned mouth and 'whiskers' of the barbel family. They are numerous in most canals but are not often seen, except in the clearest of water. The back is usually mottled brown in colour, with flanks of bluish-silver. The tail is forked. They have only two barbules on the lip. They are not big fish. A gudgeon of one or two ounces is a good fish.

Gudgeon obtain most of their food from the bottom. They often move slowly over the bottom in large shoals, gleaning scraps of food wherever they can find them. They are good bait for pike, and are important make-weight fish in matches.

Minnow *(Phoxinus phoxinus)*

These little fish are often so numerous in canals that they are classed as a pest. They are usually olive-green in colour, with flanks varying from creamy white to yellow. During the breeding season, the male acquires brilliant colours of red and gold. The female is dull-coloured, has a plump belly, and is larger in size. Unlike gudgeon, minnows shoal thickly off-bottom rather than on it. During the winter, they retire to deeper water and are not seen or caught as frequently as in the summer.

Minnows are much maligned by canal anglers, but they are valuable forage fish and very useful for bait purposes. They are easily caught with a maggot or a fragment of worm.

Stone loach *(Cobitus barbatuala)*

Similar to the gudgeon in appearance, these little fish are much smoother and are often greenish-yellow in colour. They are usually solitary, or confined to small groups, and can sometimes be seen lying on a flat stone in the shallows. They are sometimes mistaken for small barbel but are really quite different. They rarely exceed four or five inches in length. Their scales are exceedingly small, the fins are dotted or striped, and there are six barbules – two at the corners of the jaws, the others situated on the front of the lip. They can be caught in a net or with a maggot or small worm.

Stickleback *(Pygosteus pungitius)*

These tiny fish are often very numerous and undoubtedly offer serious competition for the minute organisms upon which the fry of the larger fish feed. They are usually of the three-spined variety, but are sometimes five- or even ten-spined. Despite their smallness, they are extremely tough, having horny, plated sides, and sharp spines on their backs.

During the breeding season, the males are brilliantly beautiful. The belly-colour ranges from pink to vivid scarlet and the back is jade-green, blue or a luminous shade of grey. The female stays dull but swells up remarkably, hence the nickname 'bumblebelly'. The male constructs a nest of fragments of debris and reed, and into this he drives the female of his choice to lay her eggs. He then mounts guard over the nest and stays there until the young are hatched and able to fend for themselves. During this period, the male is very aggressive and will attack larger fish if they venture near the nest.

It is difficult to say whether sticklebacks perform any useful function in a canal; but it is equally difficult to envisage how they could be eliminated, supposing such a step were desirable. Most anglers would be glad if they could be removed. On the other hand, they are small boys' fish which can be caught in a net or with the crudest of tackle, provided that the hook is small. They can even be caught without a hook if they are fished for with a worm tied to a thin line. Their greed is such that they will try to swallow the worm, and they can then often be pulled smartly from the water before they have a chance to eject it.

OTHER FISH

Trout *(Salmo trutta)*

These game fish are found in only a few canals, and usually only when the canal is a man-made link between lakes or river systems. Brown trout are smooth, and brownish-green along the back. The flanks are often tinged with gold and heavily spotted with red or purple spots. Like all members of the salmon family, they have an adipose fin – a little fin situated on the back and near to the tail. The mouth holds numerous needle-sharp teeth.

Trout will eat almost anything, from insects and their larvae to other fish, and even smaller members of their own species. A fish weighing one pound is acceptable to most anglers; but in selected waters they grow up to ten pounds. In England, the Driffield Canal is the best-known water for trout.

Grayling *(Thymallus thymallus)*

Grayling are even more uncommon in canals than trout, but they are found in the Driffield Canal. Their most distinguishing feature is undoubtedly the large, almost oval-shaped dorsal fin, which is totally different from that of any other fish. They are also covered with tiny scales which, on the flanks, gleam with a profusion of colour ranging from pure silver to mauve and pink. In shape, they are almost herring-like; and apart from the adipose fin, they bear no resemblance to any other game fish. In fact, they are not classed as game fish at all.

A grayling of a pound in weight could be called a good fish. Those caught are rarely in excess of three pounds in weight. They are truly fish of the swift, clean rivers of the north.

They feed on a wide range of insects and larvae and will often rise well to the fly, but the best baits are maggots and red-worms. They also eat other fish, and can be caught with a minnow. One of the best fish caught anywhere in recent years was taken from the Driffield Canal by Keith Hall of Kilham, Yorkshire. It weighed three and a half pounds and was taken on a worm.

Carp *(Cyprinius carpo)*

Carp are not common in canals, but they are found in some. In fact, they may be more widespread than is thought. Quite large fish of up to fifteen pounds and more in weight have been taken from a few canals. The Kennet and Avon Canal contains them. So does the Macclesfield Canal.

They are large, distinctive fish, with a thick, deep body which is usually bronze in colour. Two large and two small barbules adorn the mouth. The dorsal fin is long and has a concave edge.

Despite their size, carp feed mainly upon minute organisms and are often very difficult to tempt with a bait. Cheese, worms and bread-baits account for most of those that are caught; but a few have been taken with live-baits, flies and spinners.

Smaller, Crucian carp might sometimes be found in canals. They rarely exceed three pounds in weight. They have no barbules on the mouth, and this makes it easy to distinguish them from common carp. They, too, can be caught with worms, cheese and the bread-baits.

Index

Anglers' Library

T. C. Ivens **Still Water Fly-Fishing** 50p

'Another great classic . . . Long regarded as the standard work on still water fly-fishing . . . confirms its position as one of the world's best textbooks on angling' SCOTSMAN

'A very good book by a good, experienced and thinking fisherman. It contains much of value for the skilled and novice alike, from flies and tactics to boat handling and clothing' THE FIELD

Trevor Housby **Boat Fishing** 60p

An experienced professional charter-boat skipper describes the most productive boat-fishing techniques for salt-water species, described here, together with a wealth of practical hints.

Shark Fishing in British Waters 40p

Many varieties of shark may be found and fished within easy distance of Britain's coastline. Trevor Housby draws on a fund of shark-fishing expertise and experience to show how the use of light-tackle techniques and a sound knowledge of each individual species can place shark fishing at the top of the big-game fishing league, with its demands upon courage, endurance and skill.

You can buy these and other Pan books from booksellers and newsagents; or direct from the following address:
Pan Books, Cavaye Place, London SW10 9PG
Send purchase price plus 15p for the first book and 5p for each additional book, to allow for postage and packing
Prices applicable in UK

While every effort is made to keep prices low, it is sometimes necessary to increase prices at short notice. Pan Books reserve the right to show on covers new retail prices which may differ from those advertised in the text or elsewhere